372 · 9410

How Not to Teach

This book is due for return on or before the last date shown belc

D0300177

How Not to Teach

Mr Read

continuum

Continuum International Publishing Group

The Tower Building   80 Maiden Lane
11 York Road   Suite 704
London   New York
SE1 7NX   NY 10038

© Mr Read 2006

British Library Cataloguing-in-Publication Data
A catalogue record for this book is available from the British Library.

ISBN: 0–8264–8981–8 (paperback)

Library of Congress Cataloging-in-Publication Data
A catalog record for this book is available from the Library of Congress.

Typeset by YHT Ltd, London
Printed and bound in Great Britain by Cromwell Press, Trowbridge, Wilts

Contents

Summer

Conclusion

Introduction

1 The heirs of M'Choakumchild

How not to teach? Charles Dickens in *Hard Times* (1854) began the novel with a coruscating attack on rote learning. The second chapter, 'Murdering the Innocents', is set in Thomas Gradgrind's bleak, utilitarian school, where only facts are sacred. We are introduced to the teacher Mr M'Choakumchild, 'If he had only learnt a little less, how infinitely better he might have taught much more!' How could the heirs of M'Choakumchild proceed to recreate this dystopia?

They could start by:

- narrowing the curriculum to concentrate on English, maths and science. Sideline any fripperies like art, music, reading for enjoyment, teachers will be 'loaded to the muzzle with facts, and prepared to blow them clean out of the regions of childhood at one discharge'.
- telling teachers exactly what, where, when and how they should teach. Take all control or autonomy of the curriculum away from them, turn them into mere functionaries, automatons who will faithfully impart the lesson plans from a centralized office.
- making schools into another link in the chain that is ruthlessly driven by that office, strip them of any initiative or power to innovate.
- constantly testing and retesting children, so they are 'ready to have imperial gallons of facts poured into them until they were full to the brim'.
- burying schools and teachers in a blizzard of papers, circulars, memos, forms, documents, questionnaires.

In schools that inhabit a latter-day Coketown, thrust the blade of the knife up to the hilt and twist by implementing the following:

- instituting a punitive inspection regime that targets schools and teachers in these areas for failure. The inspector would always have 'a system to force down the general throat like a bolus . . . bore his opponent . . . and was certain to knock the wind out of common sense'.
- compiling league tables for tests with the certain knowledge that these schools will languish at the bottom.
- organizing a system of school funding to reward those with full classes.
- publicly 'naming and shaming' those schools who fail to perform – 'poverty is no excuse'.

I came late to teaching. Like many others before and since I started helping out in my children's school and got the bug for teaching, I knew I could relate to children. I've taught for nearly ten years in the same school, some of my experiences every teacher can relate to, others may be unique – poor leadership, teaching in an economically 'challenged' (aka poor) area, a results-obsessed LEA, constant pressure to improve results. The strain affects schools in different ways, I've seen three neighbouring schools implode – one closing, a staff mutiny at another and the headteacher resigning.

During my teacher training, I caught the beginning of the new Ofsted-inspired courses. It's far worse now, trainee teachers are familiar with schemes of work, can write long-term, medium-term and short-term lesson plans, are able to write detailed daily plans and will have to spend hours assessing every lesson taught in minute detail. They will have been force-fed grammar, overdosed on verbs, adjectives and nouns and gorged on targets and objectives. But after three years' training they may well know nothing about child development theories, will not have been given any art or music tuition, cannot put gym equipment out safely and are ignorant about the process of writing. M'Choakumchild and 'some one hundred and forty other schoolmasters had been lately turned at the same time, in the same factory, on the same principles, like so many piano-forte legs'.

Teacher-training courses have one of the highest dropout rates and even of those who do qualify a high proportion don't even make it into the profession. Then there's the reality check of teaching, within five years somewhere between a half and a third leave. It can be even harder for young teachers in primary schools, a bad placement you only have to endure for a few weeks. You've spent your whole life with young people at school and college and then you're marooned in a school with a bunch of morose, stressed-out 50-somethings (half of teachers will retire within 10 years) with no social life on the brink of retirement. One teacher I knew had a large number on the wall in front of his desk – 1,947 one day, the next 1,946 ... he was counting down the days to retirement.

For men there's the added problem of being an endangered species, 20 years ago a quarter of primary teachers were men, it's now down to 13 per cent, and even though they've tried to attract more recruits only 1 in 8 of trainees are male. In an era when many children are brought up solely by their mothers, men seem to shirk the responsibility, it's a shame there is a lack of male role models in schools.

The nature of the job has completely changed, in years gone by they were like *Blue Peter* presenters, always ready with sticky-backed plastic (only years later did I discover in the time before product placement it was Sellotape) – 'here's one I prepared earlier'. Who can forget the Advent and Christmas calendars, the fluffy pom-poms made from wool and cardboard, that vast collection of pets – now banned under health and safety rules. The model teacher would now be akin to a semi-desiccated calculating machine, a targets-driven workaholic. I read one report about a headteacher who had given every child targets to reach, set up dartboards in every class and in his office, 'We live in a target-driven culture'. To quote Mr Gradgrind, 'You must use combinations and modifications ... which are susceptible of proof and demonstration. This is the new discovery. This is fact.'

There's a massive gulf between secondary and primary teaching. In primary you're trying to master 10 or 11 different subjects. There's the familiarity (or not) of a small staff team. In Ireland all teachers are in one union, I met a headteacher who was employed as a mediator. The worst case he'd come across was a small school with two staff, and for ten years they hadn't spoken to each other, the only method of communication was exchanging notes via the part-time secretary.

There's sometimes that resistance to change, 'we've always done it this way'. Teachers who hoard supplies in their own classroom while the school is denuded of stock. You can become isolated in your own classroom like a Japanese 'hiki-komori' who never ventures out, or the Allan Ahlberg poem about the teacher who lived in her classroom drinking the goldfish's water. It's strange how children have no perception or understanding of you outside the classroom that you are married, have children, go shopping, live a normal life. You see children outside school and they freeze.

Primary schools are also susceptible to 'mad headteacher syndrome'. In one school the headteacher communicated through a constant stream of typewritten memos, at least six a day. Eventually one teacher began to send out samizdat memos that mimicked the real thing, it caused such confusion that the headteacher was forced into storming around the school. Later he filched some headed notepaper from the council and sent the headteacher a spoof letter complaining about the enormous amount of paper used in the school. He spent weeks trying to track the official down, a Mr W.A.S. Teit. A friend of mine was training in a country school where the headteacher lived in the school and used to take the assembly in her dressing gown and then retired to her study for the rest of the morning.

Secondaries have cultural landmarks created by books, TV and films – *The Prime of Miss Jean Brodie*, *Please Sir*, *Kes*, *To Sir with Love*, *Grange Hill*, *Teachers*, *The Simpsons* and the lovelorn Mrs Krabappel. *Tom Brown's Schooldays*, Jennings and Darbyshire and Harry Potter have represented public schools.

There's just no equivalent for primary schools, there's only Miss Read's 'Village School', another universe away from my experience, or Gervaise Phinn's heart-warming and whimsical tales about the Yorkshire Dales. What spoilt it for me was when I discovered that he was a former Ofsted inspector, as soon as I hear those words ... it's like concentration camp guard, wife-beater, estate agent, the empathy instantly disappears.

The French have excelled in film, there was *It All Starts Today* (1999) set in a former mining town. Daniel Lefebvre is an idealistic principal of a primary school and a would-be writer. He struggles to do his best for his young charges but is constantly thwarted by the incompetence or indifference of the regional authorities, the hostility of his superiors and the apathy or despair of the parents themselves. His tendency to rage at bureaucrats brings down on him a school inspection. Meanwhile, his ex-miner father suffers a near-fatal stroke. The sullen son of his girlfriend Valéria helps some thugs break into the primary school to vandalize it. She resents his apparent unwillingness to give her another child. One of the parents kills herself and her children with an overdose of phenobarbital. It's not all doom and gloom, there is an uplifting ending.

Etre et Avoir (2003) was a fly-on-the-wall documentary about a single-class French village school, in a remote Auvergne farming community. The dozen-or-so pupils – boys and girls whose ages ranged from four to ten – were all taught by a dedicated and caring teacher, Georges Lopez, who was approaching retirement. There were lessons in the basics of reading, writing, and mathematics, but there were also more playful activities – such as making pancakes, tobogganing in the snow, and picnicking in the summer fields. They learnt how to get along peacefully with one another – verbal and physical disputes were settled by reasoned discussion, not through physical chastisement – and they were encouraged to express their fears and worries.

We certainly haven't emulated that in any branch of the media. There tends to be the 'My thirty years as head of xxxx primary school', but very few books that reflect the reality of teaching or that raise their heads out of the trenches. There's a plethora of helpful handbooks, manuals and books that tell you how to do this or that, texts that give teachers advice on how to cope with the long hours, stress or poor behaviour. Very few seem to ask the question – why? Neither do they have any historical perspective that charts the changes and developments that have changed the landscape of primary teaching, with all the force and destructiveness of a tsunami.

I've tried to tell it as it is, warts and all, the plain, unvarnished truth. Obviously the charge will be levelled, why the cloak of anonymity? One of the problems is that in our culture the whistle blower, the person who has the courage to shout 'The emperor has no clothes!' is liable to find themselves out of a job. We don't have an LEA that is open to critical debate. I really feel this is a story waiting to be told, prospective teachers need to know the truth, many teachers will identify with this book and those deserters from the front (by retirement or resignation) might raise a weary smile.

Teachers who have studied Montessori and Steiner, or read about Summerhill know there is another way. Unfortunately Gradgrind and M'Choakumchild have leapt from the pages of fiction to control our schools. 'What I want is Facts. Teach these boys and girls nothing but Facts. Facts alone are wanted in life. Plant nothing else, and root out everything else. You can only form the minds of reasoning animals upon Facts: nothing else will ever be of service to them.' That's how not to teach.

2 Some history ... how did it ever come to this?

1926 and 1931

The Hadow reports call for the establishment of separate primary and secondary schools. The primary curriculum is described in terms of 'activity and experience', but also acknowledges the importance of 'facts to be stored'.

1944

The Education Act formalizes selection through the 11-plus exam with the creation of grammar and secondary modern schools (during the 1950s one in eight children from the former went to university – in the latter only one in 22,000). To prepare children for exams the primary curriculum is dominated by reading, writing and number. Classes are frequently streamed into different ability sets.

1967

After three years of intensive study, the Plowden Report recommends the expansion of nursery education, mixed-ability teaching and the extension of progressive teaching methods. It calls for 'special stress on individual discovery, on first-hand experience and on opportunities for creative work'. Reading it I felt like a survivor on a dusty, barren, post-apocalyptic planet who finds a secret book and discovers there used to be meadows, rivers and birds that sang – but he has inherited the wasteland.

1976

Three events challenge progressive teaching –

1) The Auld Report criticizes teachers at William Tyndale Junior School, in London, for adopting an extreme version of child-centred education.
2) Neville Bennett publishes *Teaching Styles and Pupil Progress*, which claims that formal teaching styles produce better test results.
3) Labour Prime Minister James Callaghan in a speech at Ruskin College attacks, 'new and informal methods of teaching'.

1988

The Conservative government finally tackles primary education. The Education Reform Act establishes a national curriculum, tests at 7 and 11 years of age, league tables, local management of schools and allows parents to choose a school outside their local education authority.

1992

The Three Wise Men's Report (Woodhead, Alexander and Rose) claims that 'the progress of primary pupils has been hampered by the influence of highly questionable dogmas...'
Ofsted is established, to oversee the inspection of schools.

1997

The Labour government reappoints Chris Woodhead as Chief Inspector of Ofsted, and announces that testing and league tables will continue. More central direction of the curriculum continues with the Literacy Hour and Numeracy Strategy.

1999

The Moser Report, *Improving Literacy and Numeracy: A Fresh Start*, sets out the National Literacy Strategy and introduces National Learning Targets. This represents a considerable increase in government interference in the curriculum.

Whereas the Tories had told teachers *what* to teach, Labour is now telling them *how* to teach it.

2000

The creeping privatization of the education service takes another step forward when it is announced that consultants would be sent into the LEAs in Bradford, Rochdale and Waltham Forest to advise on how improvements could be made after Ofsted uncovered 'serious weaknesses' in their work.

Ofsted's Chief Inspector Chris Woodhead resigns.

2001

Following the general election, Estelle Morris takes over from David Blunkett as Secretary of State for Education.

2002

Estelle Morris resigns when test results fail to reach targets.

Bowing to pressure from the teacher unions and others, new Education Secretary Charles Clarke announces that primary school tests and targets would be streamlined. The tests for 7 year olds would be less formal and would form part of a wider teacher-led assessment.

2004

In December, Ruth Kelly is appointed Education Secretary.

2005

In May, Ruth Kelly is replaced by Alan Johnson.

3 Drowning not waving – teaching in an 'economically challenged area'

Drowning people are often mistaken for someone waving. By this time, the victim is too tired to thrash about frantically, it's just a limp attempt to signal for help. People watching often fail to recognize the signs.

Half of all teachers leaving in five years, or finding an easier school at the first opportunity? No surprise to us. Those teachers able to join the escape committee notice the difference straight away. Last year, one of our teachers left to join a 'Miss Read'-style village school, she had four parent-helpers in her class – two of them with PhDs. Worried about the Key Stage 1 SATs results, the head told her 'Don't worry, just get the parents to help the children at home'. Rather than sorting out conflicts between children she spent time teaching, there was only one playground incident in the first term, when one child was called 'thick'. The school organized fencing lessons, foreign languages, skiing trips and boasted a parent-run website and library.

It's only then do you realize what a struggle it is in our school. It's not just the wider issues – behaviour, the rigid curriculum, league tables – it's those smaller things; the home reading books, only half ever returned; the homework dutifully completed by 7 out of a class of 30; the permission letters which run into the second or third issue (even then we'll make two or three phone calls on the day of the trip); the parents' evening where only half attend.

The main problem is that growing hardcore of problem children who are just refusing to conform/are persistently violent/run out of class or school/refuse to work in class and distract other children. In our small school we have about ten children who would fit into the problem category. There are days when you feel overwhelmed, because there're also the other children with behavioural problems, short attention spans or learning difficulties. It's that question of critical mass – a school with well-motivated children and supportive parents is almost bound to succeed. Start from the opposite premise and you're battling against the odds.

An example of just how tough it is teaching in some of the crumbling inner-city schools comes from Manchester's own research – 85 per cent of teachers leave the city or the profession within five years.

The local context is bleak, when the main employer closed during the 1980s the town went into a spiral of decline. People worked in the factory at dirty and dangerous jobs for low pay, but at least there was stability, a reason to get up in the morning and a sense of achievement, there were also numerous sporting and social organizations attached to the factory.

I sometimes feel that we've lost a generation, the grand-parents seem more organized in their lives and have greater aspirations for their grandchildren. The factory work has been replaced by the McJobs – we used to make things. There's also that other social phenomenon – the sink estate, people who do get jobs move away (our area has one of the highest emigration rates in the country) leaving estates full of the old or unemployed.

The changes to the education system also eat through our school like a long-term lingering cancer. One example is local management of schools, or to put it crudely, you get paid for bums on seats, once you have falling school rolls you're always struggling for cash and that goes on for years – evidence the dog-eared books, peeling paint work, frayed gym mats.

Schools in the suburbs with full classes are not only blessed with well-motivated children but with the money. Some Parent Teacher Associataions (PTAs) raise substantial sums for those little extras – we struggle to raise a few hundred pounds from the bingo. My friend's school was setting out to raise £10,000 from parents for a new playground with a sponsored parachute jump.

There's also the way our society has developed over the last 25 years, the 'greed is good' culture elbowed children aside – in 1979 10 per cent of children were brought up in poverty, by 1997 the figure was one third, even years of effort from New Labour has only reduced that to 25 per cent. It's not only material poverty (try asking some of our children what they did in the holidays – 'nothing') it's poverty of hope. One of our classroom assistants was walking back with one of our bright Year 6s from McDonald's (they'd won the house points competition, OK, we're a healthy eating school but you have to make some concessions). She asked her what she wanted to do when she left school, the answer, 'lie on the couch all day and watch the soaps' – she wasn't joking.

One of the current mantras is 'joined-up thinking', yet whenever we approach an outside agency for help, somehow the system fails to work. We referred one of our children (constantly banging his head on the table, self-harming) to the school psychiatric service, back came the reply a few weeks later which roughly translated said 'we're under-funded, under-staffed, join the queue, but don't get your hopes up'. Or the speech-therapy sessions which we refer children to – if the parents don't keep the appointments the children are removed from the list.

The pressure from league tables is constant, one of our few downwardly mobile parents said recently 'Justin's grandmother saw the League Tables in the paper and wants to know what he's doing at such an awful school' – yeah, thanks for that.

I'm not trying to claim that teachers and schools don't make a difference – parental help is seven times more important for children's progress than social class. There used to be a crude determinism that poor children were bound to fail. The problem is that the school improvement ideology ignored social class and reduced progress to a crude set of input and output measures – a simple bullet-point list. Then we had the trite slogans, 'Poverty is not an excuse', 'Zero tolerance of failure'.

Schools used to work together, now the creation of an education market has locked neighbouring schools in mutual rivalry, competition for children is fierce – would Tesco help out Sainsbury's? Rather than schools sharing expertise, cooperating and supporting each other, they exist as self-sufficient islands – our neighbouring schools? They might as well be on Mars.

Allied to this process has been the change and decline of the Local Education Authorities, the Conservatives wanted to abolish them, Labour has allowed them to wither on the vine. We used to have advisers for all the curriculum subjects, there used to be training sessions, coordinators' meetings. Now it's been narrowed down to English, maths and science. We have school improvement officers, whose main function is to haul schools up the SATs league table. The pressure on headteachers is unrelenting – and they wonder why so many posts are readvertised?

Schools and teachers in poor areas used to get extra money – during the Thatcherite counter-revolution this ended and schools started from Year Zero. Money has gone into recruiting thousands of classroom assistants of varying quality – no surprise there given the minimal training they often receive. Contrast that with Finland where every teacher has the equivalent of an MA. The narrowest gap in achievement based on social class is in the Scandinavian countries, there social mobility is still the norm. In Britain even by the age of 22 months a gap has opened between children. When they leave school, a middle-class child is 15 times more likely to replicate his/her class origins compared to the chances of a working-class child breaking out of his/her class background.

Sometimes it's one incident that brings it home to you. Recently we were going by coach to our local secondary school for a PE day. We stopped off at another primary school (Free School Meals (FSM) 5 per cent) their children filed out of the gate. Our children always wear an assortment of PE tops, and usually 5 or 6 forget and wear the school cast-offs. At this school every child wore a freshly ironed PE top with the school crest emblazoned on it, all were wearing the latest trainers. One child was without his kit, but this was soon remedied by his mother who stepped onto the coach with a brand new tracksuit and trainers. I just sat there open-mouthed, maybe our kids noticed, possibly not, they didn't comment, but wait till they get to secondary school – they'll just be the povos.

It's that fatal combination of factors – Britain's crumbling urban estates, poverty, the education market, parents struggling to cope, demotivated children, league tables – that's why we're drowning not waving.

An edited version of this article first appeared in The Times Edu-cational Supplement.

Autumn

4 Snake oil – the training day

As soon as I hear the words 'Training Day', the default in my memory retrieves that brilliant episode from *The Office* – 'there's a fox, a chicken and a bag of grain, a man has a boat . . .' After that a new template has been set, it's been redefined. Somehow *The Office* also chimed with the zeitgeist, after Blair's talk about business leaders being 'heroes' we had Enron, Railtrack and World Com. It also mimicked and subverted the docusoap TV programmes, I loved the Easyjet ones where an irate businessman who had missed his flight would demand to see 'the person in charge'. A customer relations manager (usually some pimply faced youth) would give the standard reply, 'We're a budget airline, if you don't like us go elsewhere'.

Training days seem to be full of the bland, the inconsequential, and the downright trite, if I hear 'think outside the box' again I swear I'll inflict irreparable injuries. One day the trainer put up a great big blue screen,

'What's this?'

'A big blue screen.'

No, of course, it was a whale! We had to stand back and look at the bigger picture! Yeah, right.

The thought of a training day to start the school year wasn't exactly inspiring, the LEA sessions usually consist of various consultants handing down the tablets of stone straight from the DfES manuals. One of them actually said, 'If the Literacy Hour is designed by a man in an office in London and every school follows it to the letter, I don't have a problem with that.'

This time all the teachers in the authority have been gathered together for a session on Accelerated Learning with 'Mr Motivator', Alistair Smith. Going into the hall I meet all my colleagues and we swap holiday stories, moan about the children and anticipate the start of school. I bump into Pat and the teachers from St Kevin's, they're having a really hard time, the

SATs scores are the lowest in the area, they've had continual visits from the LEA hit squad, the head has been forced out and the new one is there to lick the school into shape.

Alistair Smith proves to be a really witty and inspiring speaker, the sort you could listen to all day, if he ever tried it as a stand-up comedian he'd make a fortune. He's pioneering this new system called Accelerated Learning. The idea is that children use visual, auditory or kinaesthetic (VAK) styles of learning and as teachers we have to recognize which children use particular styles and change our teaching methods accordingly.

In the dinner break I talk to the St Kevin's teachers, like us they're in an 'economically challenged' area, with most children on FSM or special education needs (SEN). The authority has poured in consultants and shredded morale, experienced staff have been told to rewrite all the maths and English schemes of work. The worst time was when they were sent to the authority's pet school in the middle-class enclave (FSM 3 per cent) to watch an English lesson. It didn't start well, yes they were super-sensitive but they were greeted with a look and condescending smile from the head that seemed to say, 'Welcome crap teachers from the failing school on the scummy council estate, we will show you how to teach.'

They watched a lesson where the children displayed a sophistication, knowledge, depth of reading and articulation that was completely removed from all but a handful of pupils in their own classes. They also sat completely still for half an hour – not one discipline problem, no one fighting, moving out of their place, talking or interrupting. At the end they asked the teacher to come and teach a lesson in their school, needless to say they haven't got back to them!

Talking to other teachers who have used Accelerated Learning, it's not an each-way bet. The problem is that children can be placed in rigid groups – visual, auditory or kinaesthetic. One school even stuck labels on every child's desk to identify them. However, in another, the teacher tested them for learning styles at the start of the year and found that by the end of the year many of them had changed their learning style.

The LEA are really keen on it and are spending thousands to

roll it out to every school, with the expectation that opportunities for children to use VAK learning styles will be identified on all planning sheets. I'm breathless, I can't wait.

In the afternoon session there seems to be an over-concentration on improving mnemonic learning, for me it's beginning to veer towards the snake-oil salesman. 'All new Accelerated Leaning! You know it works! Guaranteed to raise your SATs scores!' There's talk about 'chunking' information as though the learning process can be reduced to handy little parcels for children to pick up along the way. There are plenty of good suggestions about giving children space, playing music, encouraging them to drink water so they don't become dehydrated. But I'm left wondering why the LEA has thrown hundreds of teachers into a cramped, hot, stuffy hotel room with no time for breaks.

The central message is that individual teachers can make a difference – that's fine, no argument there, but it also depends on the social context and setting of the school. I'm also concerned that in a whole day, no time has been allotted for teachers to ask questions, imagine if we did that in the classroom.

We've listened all day to a brilliant speaker, learned that children need to drink a lot of water and posters work best where they stimulate the left side of the brain, but some of us are asking, 'Where's the Beef?'

5 'A local school for local people' – managing a class

The Sunday before school starts, I spend the day walking around Hadfield on the outskirts of Greater Manchester, aka Royston Vasey, the setting for *The League of Gentlemen*. You wait ages for a decent comedy and not only are there those gothic monstrosities, but *The Office* and *Phoenix Nights* come along as well. Fans and aficionados share those quips and catchphrases like some secret society that is impenetrable to those outside. When our school was looking for a motto, our former head was ready to choose mine – 'A Local School for Local People'.

It's always strange coming back after the long summer break, you forget the codes to the doors, it takes a while to get your brain back into the old routines. You start to live for the holidays – the teacher's mantra really is 'Christmas, Easter, Summer ... Christmas, Easter, Summer ...' It can take ages to wind down on holiday, then you get the smart remarks about 'all those holidays'. Try teaching, pal. At the end of summer you do miss the good kids, the funny exasperating ones, the strange and the odd, but not the downright cheeky, the mentally unbalanced or the child who should have had a screen test for *The Omen*.

Coming back this year I know it's a 'difficult' class. It's strange how most classes settle from nursery onwards and travel through the school largely without modification. In this case, five or six problem children have been added to a class that has been hard to control. I know from experience that a bad class, is a bad class, is a bad class. That feeling of why can't I cope? When I was a supply teacher some classes were a breeze, others a total nightmare. All you can do is use your tried-and-trusted methods.

It's back to the grind of planning, losing that chunk of Sunday. We had a session from a consultant on 'getting your weekend back'. The solution? Her friend's school, where all the teachers stayed in school until 9 o'clock on a Thursday night. Yeah, thanks, but no thanks. We started with A4 planning sheets for maths and English, we progressed to A3 sheets; irony was lost on her when I suggested using A2 size.

Before considering how to manage a class it's important to put it in context, there are the constraints or the straitjacket of the prescriptive national curriculum where 70 per cent of time is for English, maths and science. What if you've got a potential dancer, musician, artist, footballer or explorer? They're bound to get frustrated. Heads are under pressure for results, and the personality of the head has a decisive influence in primary schools, they may be liberal and tolerant, leaving some decisions to the professional judgement of their teachers, down to the micro-managers who want to dictate the colour of the wall displays.

Most important is the social context of the school and the attitude of parents – a class full of motivated children with supportive parents in a well-resourced school – teaching is so much easier. Start from the opposite premise and you've got problems.

I hate some of the trite slogans or sayings about classroom management; the worst must be designed for robots or control freaks, 'Don't smile until Christmas'. True, with some classes it's 'How to avoid a nervous breakdown before half-term', but hey, most classes – they're just young children. Treat them like terrorists and they'll act like terrorists. There's also the Dos and Don'ts list mentality, OK, don't shout, but when you make a simple request for the sixth time on a Friday afternoon ... you're only human. And some classes would try the patience of Mother Teresa, Buddha and Nanny 911.

There are of course many absolutes – what makes a good teacher? Fairness, kindness, respect, knowledge, praise and high expectations. Similarly, classroom management depends on good preparation, timing, pace, questioning skills and setting the right level of work. However, what works with one class won't with another, each teacher is different. The skill is in knowing what will work for your particular class.

The dynamics of a class is another chance factor that can be difficult to alter or change. Which children set the tone in the class? One class I had a very mature set of girls, as soon as one of the boys started playing up they'd shout out 'Shut up Barry don't be pathetic!' It helped that I got on with them, but other classes the girls could be silent and timid. Getting the class quiet before break can be problematic, one class I had, at 10.30 there would be absolute silence because all the boys wanted to get out and play football. On the other hand, some classes have no cohesion or unity of purpose as Marx said about the French peasantry, 'everyone a different shape and size'.

Some classes you have to really boss and show them you mean business. But in all cases you have to set minimum standards, without being fussy or allowing for disabilities or differences. Teachers can get fanatical about presentation, yes it's important but many left-handed children struggle early on. You have a great opportunity to know all the quirks and idiosyncrasies of children by working with them all year, an advantage over secondary teachers. On the other hand they know there's only one lesson a week with 10E.

Primary children are still of an age where they love, adore and hoard stickers, certificates and awards. They like it when you talk about your own family. You also have to be flexible, last few minutes of the day, read a story, play some music (one class were hooked on my Johnny Cash CD), dancing, a few jokes, play outside on the yard, in other words you're trying to create an atmosphere. But don't get me wrong, for some classes, none of the above would be possible.

The first day and week allow you to get a feel for the class, you'll have a good idea from the previous teacher. But sometimes the monster from last year is an angel for you, or vice versa. Seating arrangements can be vital; again you're constrained by the Literacy Hour, which insists that children are seated on tables in ability groups. I try to get children to write something about themselves – likes, dislikes; what positive rules they want in the class; why learning is important. I also spend time just watching how they interact with each other, sometimes you need to move children if they don't get on together.

Empathy and understanding are important qualities in a teacher, trying to reach out to every child as difficult as it may be in some cases. You look for something in each child that you can nurture and develop. The home background for many children is often horrendous, you have to take that into account without excusing bad behaviour.

The first week is important to assess children's ability without going overboard on testing, but in our school the hardest part is teaching the different levels in the class. Some children will be two years behind, others two years ahead. In maths you may be teaching simple addition as opposed to seven-figure numbers, in English, an accomplished short-story writer compared to others who are still sequencing the alphabet.

There's a cheesy mug that lists the different jobs that a teacher has to engage with – social worker, administrator, referee, etc. The main skill is being like a conductor, but you're trying to control 30 different instruments not all necessarily working from the same song sheet. There's also a large element of being an actor, treading the boards in front of an audience and not losing them. However, you're not entirely working from a script, you have to think on your feet all the time. Be prepared for the unexpected, it may be that the class has gone out to play and its been windy, or there's a plague of daddy long legs, or a wasp flies into the classroom.

Parents can be an important support, but there are different pressures in different schools. In the leafy suburbs it might be why Johnny or Jemima hasn't become a PhD yet. Some parents don't give children clear boundaries, spoil them too much or over-react, 'I've been grounded for a month'. Getting them working with you and your school is crucial. Thankfully the professional elitism and isolation that said to parents 'don't come past the gate' has long gone.

You have to keep believing that you can make a difference to children's lives. It's that wellspring of hope and optimism; it's just that we have to keep digging deeper every year.

6 Not the *Caine Mutiny* – the headteacher leaves

Erica's called a special staff meeting after school; the smart money is on the brown envelope from Ofsted (we're due another inspection). Thoughts also wander from that to the bizarre – she's going to tell us what wonderful teachers we are, to the extreme – we're going to get new desks for the children (at parents' evening they can still point to where they carved their names). Erica closes all the doors in the staffroom, and in a hushed whisper informs us that she's resigning and the LEA are sending her off on a jolly forthwith, maintenant, she'll be gone by Christmas. There's a collective intake of breath, I can see that everyone wants to jump up and down, cheer, sing hosannas, break out the bunting, let off firecrackers. But being teachers, we sit there expressionless, significantly, no one says 'STAY!'

You'd have to describe Erica's management style as 'hands-off'. You'd go for weeks and realize the only time you'd seen her was at the unplanned chaotic staff meeting, or in one of the interminable assemblies. She'd usually disappear into her office first thing, and in the afternoon, as you stayed on marking and stapling up displays, you'd see her sports car breaking the brow of the hill. Every Monday morning you'd look at the week's events and almost inevitably it would be 'Thursday, Friday – Erica out on a course'.

Naturally, Erica inhabited some kind of parallel universe where she really believed that it was only her inspiring leadership that stopped the school from imminent collapse and catastrophe – definitely a case of false consciousness. She'd never teach, if you sent any badly behaved children to her, she'd have a little talk, they'd come back with a sticker and be worse than ever. If you sent any children's work to her for praise, it would come back with a comment about how they had to move on to some impossible target that was out of reach, like DUH! You must be a dim teacher not to spot that.

When I first started on supply I had a boy in class called Marvin who used to beat the other children up. I found him one day holding another child by the scruff of the neck and banging the door handle into his forehead. Erica told me he was so 'sorry'. I realized then that if Marvin actually succeeded in terminating any children, Erica would possible give him a dinnertime detention. On the other hand, when Malcolm told her to 'F-off' he got suspended for a week.

One of the little rituals was the morning briefing where Erica would open her post and read out the letters. There was a classic one involving a correspondent from Canada who was obviously displaying the initial signs of dementia. Condensing the five-page letter (Erica insisted on inflicting all five pages on us) the man had lived in the area 25 years ago and had bought a brick in the school building appeal, as he had now fallen on hard times, could he have it back? Eventually I began to find excuses to miss the 'morning briefing' or just forgot to attend, and by popular acclaim it eventually became redundant.

At the end of every term we had that tiresome ritual, the end-of-term meal. When we were called to take our seats in the restaurant, Erica would stride to the head of the table, behind her would be a queue of teachers jostling to get to the back, if you sat next to her you'd get a monologue about sports cars, designer clothes, exotic holidays – basically me, myself and I. She'd never ask anyone about themselves or their family.

You'd have to say that the health, welfare and professional development of teachers was never exactly top of her agenda, as long as there was a warm body to throw in front of a class that was enough. However, in the depths of winter even that basic task would elude her, the coal-fired boiler would continually break down, leaving you and the children shivering in the class with coats on. Naturally, Erica's room was the coldest in the school.

Her lack of preparation was always evident when it came to school assemblies. Erica would insist on inflicting her rambling, incoherent, heart-warming and uplifting stories on the children and staff. I became the official timekeeper, and the record was logged on a Thursday morning at 27 minutes 23 seconds.

You could say she wasn't the best team player. One

Christmas we'd all spent hours putting up the Christmas dec-
orations, some of the classroom assistants had been labouring
away since dinnertime. We stood back and admired the lan-
terns, grotto and tree. Just then Erica appeared, strolled round
the hall and watched as the last few streamers were attached to
the wall. She informed us that they were bound to fall down,
we weren't putting them up correctly, she'd been on a course
on display and you had to form the Blu-Tack into pyramids and
apply gentle pressure. It was all we could do to stop one of the
classroom assistants from garrotting her.

Our school wasn't exactly well known, you'd go on a course
and tell other teachers where you were from and they'd gaze at
you in bemusement as though you were from some obscure star
cluster in the outer reaches of Andromeda. Once, after Erica
had been on another of her courses she'd been really inspired by
a talk about a new reading scheme and she invited all the other
heads in the area to come to our school and listen to a talk,
several of them were late because they had got lost trying to
find our school. We all gathered in the school hall, it wasn't a
brilliant start because one of the more generously proportioned
headteachers sat on one of our rickety chairs, which immediately gave way underneath her. Inevitably the PowerPoint
presentation and the film failed to work, the presenter mum-
bled her way through an uninspiring talk while her assistant
frantically grappled with wires and sockets. Eventually the film
struggled into action, it was one of those hyperactive presenters
who you normally find on American television, enthusing
about how a fridge will change your life. All the participating
schools reported implausible advances in reading and there was
a fiendishly difficult recording system that would have taken
hours to use for each child. None of the authors in the reading
scheme were exactly household names. It became obvious we
were being sold a pup. One by one, the local headteachers
would rise arthritically from their chairs, look at Erica, tap their
watch and indicate towards the door. They'd leave in that
peculiar way that people leave meetings early, tiptoeing out,
hunched up, as though they were trying to avoid crunching any
twigs in the act of stalking a deer in a dark forest. Unfortunately
the exit was right next to the projector and a succession of

ghostly shadows flitted behind the screen – looking for deer. Esme from the nursery got a bad fit of the giggles and when the lights went up only our staff were left; not to worry, the buffet lasted us for days afterwards.

The last day of term just spoke volumes about Erica's capability as a manager and her empathy with staff and children. She hijacked the Year 6 leavers' assembly and rambled on for ages about her Year 5 cycling proficiency scheme, how we thrilled as they wheeled their bikes on stage. Then she began to hand out all the certificates she'd forgotten to hand out during the term, after an hour or so I reminded her about the end of year staff v pupils netball match. No, we'd have to cancel it, we hadn't done a fire drill all year, we needed to fit that in. At the end of the day we had a presentation for Leanne who had been on a temporary contract, Erica wished her luck for the future and hoped she'd find another job. Leanne smiled at her, 'I got one – a month ago'. We all knew ages ago, but Erica hadn't had the decency to enquire. I went back to class, got my bag, tidied up the class, as I was walking out I saw a nervous group of people in the staffroom clutching files, she'd left the interviews for classroom assistants until 4 pm on the last day of term.

We had a succession of capable deputy headteachers who, as well as teaching in a class, effectively ran the school. Every time I looked at the staff job descriptions I used to wonder – apart from opening the post what *exactly* does Erica do?

It didn't exactly reach the stage of the *Caine Mutiny*, that film where Humphrey Bogart plays Captain Queeg, the eccentric ship's captain who is obsessed with the stolen strawberries, and has a peculiar habit of spinning two marbles in his hand. Eventually at the height of a typhoon when the ship is going to founder, the officers remove him as captain. The other film must be *Mutiny on the Bounty* when a hysterical Trevor Howard confronts the super-cool Marlon Brando, 'Mutiny, Mr Christian? MUTINY!' 'Er well ... yes, old boy.' I've just got this picture of Erica filing her nails in the prow while the remnants of the loyal crew row the lifeboat to safety.

7 Guided reading – a boring LEA training session

There are certain moments when the fog descends and you begin to mentally construct that resignation letter. There was one this week at the Key Stage 2 guided reading course.

The LEA literacy 'consultants' (great word that) have become the gatekeepers, or more accurately the *gauleiters*, of the national literacy strategy, they torture teachers by boring them into submission and compliance.

We were lectured at for four and half hours, with only a brief intermission, for one of the infamous DfES teaching videos. This time it was a Year 5 class from Upper Middle Class Primary, Stockbroker-on-Thames, recorded in a guided reading session, discussing F. R. Leavis's critique of existentialism in Jean-Paul Sartre's novels ... oh all right I've made up the last bit, but you get the drift.

There was no attempt to engage in dialogue or debate (apart from a cursory ten minutes at the beginning) with the 30 teachers in attendance. Instead, the tablets of stone were handed down. One teacher managed to comment on how he'd motivated a special needs group by reading from the S Club 7 fanzine. This was quickly skated over and it was back to the DfES-approved OHTs.

There was a wealth of talent and experience sitting there, was any attempt made to canvass opinions, enquire what problems we had encountered or how we had solved them? But then who would be interested in us? We're only the teachers, merely the technicians, and the uncritical automatons. Pat was there with the teachers from St Kevin's, I showed them the newspaper headline, 'One-third of teachers prepare to quit'.

As our 'consultant' raced through the manual there was a cursory 'Is everyone all right with that?' I'd already asked one question and I was getting that look – don't ask another one, you'll only prolong the agony.

We are constantly lectured to about using different teaching styles and trying to interest and engage with children, yet when we go on courses we are confronted by the very boring and didactic methods we are told to avoid.

The course encapsulated everything that is wrong about the NLS – schools stripped of any autonomy over the curriculum, teachers deskilled, deprofessionalized and demotivated. Here was the what, where, when, why and how of teaching – now just get on and deliver it and if the results aren't up to scratch we'll all know who to blame.

8 The stretch limo and Prince Charles's former aide – stars for a day

I'm walking out of school with some of the children to attend our very own film premiere. They're all done up to the nines in their best clothes, the girls have gone overboard with the make-up. Luke immediately spots the white stretch limousine parked outside the school gates. 'What's that there for?'

'Dunno.'

'Who's that?' He points to the chauffeur with the peaked cap.

'Dunno.'

'How are we getting up to the leisure centre.'

'Dunno.'

The chauffeur opens the door and we all pile into the plush interior, he switches on the sound system and we help ourselves to drinks from the fridge. Luke breaks out into a smile. It was more kitsch than glitz, and pricey at £100 an hour, but I knew it was something the children would never forget.

During the 1960s the electronics factory at the back of the school used to employ thousands of people; then it went into a slow inglorious decline and finally closed in the early 1990s. On the way to the swimming baths you'd go past the wasteland, some children weren't aware that a factory that teemed with people, that blasted the sound of its buzzer over the town used to be there. It had almost been erased from memory, no statue or marker of people's working lives. Half of the old site is now a retail park with McJobs, the other half still derelict. The town used to be famous for making things, the factory and town linked umbilically, synonymous with each other. Some feat that, from working class to underclass in one generation.

I was keen to preserve the memory and to show to the children that the town used to be something, to take a pride in the past and maybe look forward to the future. We approached the local museum for help and their outreach team promised to work with our children on a drama presentation. Some of the former workers came in to our class to talk about work in the factory. History can be really dry and really boring, but they had some great stories to tell.

The head office had a team of fierce uniformed commissionaires; one of the women left school at 14 and her first job was taking messages around the factory. She was with a friend in the head office and they were at the top of a spiral stairs larking around, the letter fell out of her hands and spiralled all the way down onto the desk of the commissionaire. He roared at them to come down and demanded to know their names and department, because they were – FOR IT! Her friend gave a false name; she didn't, and was terrified for weeks that this ogre would appear to confront her. One of the lorry drivers had to take a huge cable drum over to Manchester and scraped the underside of every bridge on the way and took down half the telephone wires. There was the time Spud Murphy was driving a stacker truck through the factory and a sheet of metal fell from a height and sliced his nose off.

The owners were very paternalistic (there were many sports and social clubs) – even a hospital surgery inside the factory. But it wasn't just like the Hovis commercial, people worked long hours in dirty jobs for low pay. My wife's uncle started work there in 1968 and couldn't believe how bad the conditions were; they didn't even have a canteen then, people drank tea next to their machines.

We decided to make our own documentary and interview some of the former workers. To help us with film technique we got advice from the local university media department. They came in and showed the children how to use the camera, focusing, recording sound. It's strange how even the most loquacious of people can dry up when they are interviewed and filmed, but eventually we got some good clips. The mania for painting people's boots yellow – while they were standing there, the man who always rushed off with his snack box so he could get a seat in the canteen – when he wasn't looking they nailed the box to his workbench.

Some people we met by chance, when we went to film outside the old gates we met a security guard who used to work in 'Dante's inferno' – the copper refinery. He worked 12-hour shifts, seven days a week and still found time to teach children in the town to swim.

We wanted to include some archive film of the factory when it was working, but when we contacted the regional archives there was some arcane dispute going back into the mists of time and our area couldn't get any film. Luckily one of the ex-lorry drivers had an old promotional film and footage of the factory being knocked down.

The local city learning centre gave us a lot of support in the time-consuming and laborious task of editing. We put some really good backing music on and put in the best clips with archive photographs, film and interviews. At the end I put in a clip of the derelict site with The Specials' 'Ghost Town' in the background. Harry, the former lorry driver, looked at the rusted gates, 'The biggest electronics factory in the world, reduced to this ... all gone.'

The film premiere was at the leisure centre – ironically the former works canteen. We invited parents, the former workers and some of the bigwigs from the LEA. The press came, there was a photograph in the local paper and a piece on local radio, the regional television were covering something about back-stroke being banned in a public swimming baths – can't win 'em all.

After the premiere some of the children went up to the museum, their film drama had been short-listed for a national award. One of the judges was a former aide to Prince Charles, I was longing to ask him if HRH really did have a servant to squeeze the toothpaste onto his brush, and was he as big a plonker in real life as he appeared to be on television, but like the children I was on my best behaviour. I spotted the folder with letters from the children saying why they should win and I fondly remembered that Basil Fawlty rage when I sent Karl back for the fourth time to use capital letters to start a sentence.

A week later, a letter arrives from the director for education praising 'my dedication' and that the film was an 'outstanding example of best teaching practice'. I decide to keep the letter and file it under 'I' for Insurance Policy.

9 The one-armed bandit – in praise of supply teachers

I'm writing to celebrate that forgotten army of teachers, the people without whom schools and teachers couldn't function – courses would be cancelled, classes sent home, sabbaticals revoked. Yes, let's hear it for the supply teachers! Those unsung heroes.

Like most schools we've got our regulars – ex-staff, friends, people we've picked up along the way, the proverbial safe pair of hands. You can leave them with the class safe in the knowledge that when you come back the classroom will still be there.

There's Gemma, who's left to go on supply and has known all the children since Reception class. Charlie, who tells the children outrageous fibs – like the time he played in goal for Man United and always reminds us about his enhanced pension deal. Jean, who plans everything meticulously, marks all the books and leaves copious notes.

The problem we have is with what you might call the 'irregulars' – those teachers that time and the national curriculum just forgot. Yep, those and the just plain odd.

Most supply teachers sit in the staffroom as quiet as mice, nibbling at their sandwiches, waiting for the 3.15 bell, and then hover around the office waiting to get their form signed before edging out of the door to the safety of the car park.

Some of them we remember well – there was The Talker. He sat in the staffroom with his zipped-up cardigan and the largest Tupperware box you've ever seen. The problem was he couldn't stop talking, it was just constant, drip, drip, drip like a leaking tap splattering onto a metal sink. There was no pause for breath, even the act of eating, chewing, masticating didn't stop the flow. It was an endless discharge of the inconsequential, ephemeral, irrelevant, unimportant and trivial – the worst case of logorrhoea in medical history. After a few days of this we'd never seen the staffroom empty so quickly, people found meetings to attend, trips out to the shops or money to pay in the bank. The opinion of the staff was that his wife was going crazy and had thrown him out of the house to go on supply.

Miss Jones's topographical awareness was limited. Even after a week at the end of every break she would wander down to the Junior Department, we'd have to go and find her and lead her back to the Infants. In the depths of winter she always wore a flimsy printed cotton dress and open-toed sandals, the female staff wanted to find out what hair dye she used because it was always the carrot shade of ginger. The literacy hour? Numeracy strategy? Planning? 'Oh no dear, we'll do a few sums, read a story and do some sewing.' Her strategies for classroom control were limited, even if a full-scale civil war was imminent she seemed oblivious to it. The teaching assistants were run off their feet trying to maintain order.

The most memorable supply teacher was christened 'The one-armed bandit' by one of the less politically correct members of the staff. He signalled his presence during morning break. The door burst open nearly coming off its hinges, thudding against the wall. He surveyed the assembled staff and boomed out 'Is there a woman here to make me a cup of tea?' It was like a scene from one of those Westerns – just before the gunfight, total and utter silence, tumbleweed blowing across the empty street and then the sound of the town hall bell tolling in the distance. You could have cut the atmosphere with a knife.

Within a few minutes of getting seated he'd rubbished our estate, condemned single parents and called all the children thick. He was a huge man with only one arm but he liked the way our children dealt with his disability, he said that at some schools children shied away, our children stared at him and said 'Hey mister, you've only got one arm.'

He sorted out Year 6, when Geoff Bright started messing in his desk he dumped all his books on the floor. The highlight was when he played his guitar and let the children invent verses to 'What shall we do with the drunken teacher'? Apparently Simon, the *King of the Hill* fan, used every descriptor level in the literacy strategy only it wasn't repeatable. The last we heard of him he was working further and further away from the area as his reputation preceded him.

Thankfully the 'irregulars' only appear very rarely. The other week I was off with 'flu for a day. Now I'm not sure exactly what the class did but I know that Keith got up to Stage 10 on Death Race 2000. So whenever I announce that I'm going on a course, there's always a chorus of,

'Can we have Miss Brown?'

'No, it's Mrs Arkwright.'

'Oh no! Hard work!'

10 Brian – a pupil I'll never forget

When Brian arrived at our school, you could say that he'd literally been pushed between pillar and post. He'd missed large chunks of time in school and his records were non-existent. We counted about half a dozen schools from his haphazard recall.

His sister in Year 6 was one of nature's survivors – sassy and streetwise. Brian sat in our Year 3 class bewildered and confused. It took several days to persuade him to take off his coat and hang it up in the cloakroom. The routine of school was a mystery, when everyone stood up he remained seated, and vice versa. Brian could barely read, spell, write or count, but he'd concentrate for ages – tongue out – laboriously writing his name.

A few weeks later we were doing an exercise on likes and dislikes about school. Now one thing I believe in is having monitors – it really helps in the smooth running of the class, and empowers children. They also remind me when I've forgotten to do things like taking the register, going to assembly or doing the dinners.

It's strange how you remember certain individuals – Brian Jones the over-officious pencil monitor, or Violet Smith who began that life of crime as the milk monitor. To avoid this problem I always swap the jobs every term and pair boys and girls up.

In Brian's piece of work he wrote that he liked me as a teacher, but didn't like the fact that he didn't have a job in class. Hmm. The next day we were lining up to go to assembly and the ever-helpful Jill said, 'Shall I turn the light out?' A flash of inspiration. 'I know, we need a light monitor, that's a *really* important job, it'll help save the school money . . . Brian would you like to do it?'

His face lit up, his eyes sparkled and a smile crept across his face as wide as the Runcorn Bridge. From that moment on he was the world's best light monitor, glued to that spot by the switch, waiting for the signal.

I read about another boy, who was isolated and marginalized within a new class, he built his self-esteem by spitting the highest up the school wall. Thankfully Brian was just happy being light monitor.

An edited version of this article first appeared in The Times Educational Supplement.

11 A normal afternoon – why inclusion isn't working

This is a 'normal' afternoon, afternoons are always worse. It can often take a good 20 minutes to settle the class down and resolve disputes/fights from playtime. Dawn is refusing to come back into class and one of the class assistants is trying to coax her back in. Brian is on his back, legs and arms twitching. Derek complains constantly in a loud voice about getting skitted. Eric has had another fight at playtime; it's the third time this month he's gone to live with his Nan. His Dad's a dealer, it's not the police who are the problem, it's the rival gangs axing the front door in. Billy has run out of class three times this week and is ready to blow again. Wayne is bubbling away and the acting head will have to restrain him at afternoon play. Gary is hiding under a table, 9 years old and he's three years behind academically, but there's no chance of getting him into a special school.

I wholeheartedly endorse the principle of inclusion – educating children with SEN in mainstream schools. Forty years ago they were branded as 'educationally sub-normal', shunted out of the way and forgotten. Bright children with disabilities like David Blunkett were advised to take up basket weaving. To facilitate inclusion, special schools are closing at an increasing rate. The problem is that some children cannot cope in mainstream, or they don't receive adequate support. The main question, however, is to what extent is this driven by financial considerations?

One third of my class have severe learning difficulties or behavioural problems. I have children who run out of school, climb under or on top of tables, hit other children, hit adults, refuse instructions, self-harm, teachers become desensitized, every day is a bad day – a bit like playing REM's 'Bad Day' on a loop.

In the manic rush for exam results and percentage scores SEN children are thrust aside. Schools concentrate on the

borderline children that will make all the difference. In primary
schools, millions has been invested in booster packages 'Catch
Up' and FLS, all to push children through to Level 4. Lynette
came into nursery barely able to speak, she didn't even register
in the Year 1 tests, she really blossomed in Year 6 and worked
her socks off to reach Level 3, but did this register anywhere,
with the LEA, with Ofsted? Fugedaboutit! Level 3 equals
failure.

Funding lies at the core of the drive to close special schools,
for some cost-driven LEAs 'inclusion' is a convenient politically
correct shroud. In our LEA, increasing numbers of children
were getting SEN statements and thereby qualifying for a place
in a special school or for more support in mainstream. They
solved this problem by raising the bar, as one cynic put it, 'even
if you were brain dead you wouldn't get a statement or a place
in special school'.

Statements are based on reports from educational psycholo-
gists. Last week we received the report on one of our children
who is three years behind academically, her home background
is bleak, she self-harms, hits other children and constantly runs
out of class. The ed psych's conclusion? She can cope in
mainstream. Recently one of the ed psychs retired, in an
unguarded moment he admitted that there was an informal
quota for referrals, if you went over it you were in trouble. I
know of another case where someone was on a temporary
contract and made the mistake of statementing too many
children – he didn't get the job.

Children with severe emotional or behavioural problems are
also expected to cope in mainstream. Ten years ago our LEA
had three units that catered for 50 children on long-term pla-
cements. It wasn't ideal: children could be branded as
troublemakers, few were reintegrated into mainstream and
children didn't have any well-adjusted peers to follow. At
present there are two short-term units for 16 children, as we are
in a more prosperous part of the borough we don't have anywhere to place children. The only assistance we can call on is a
weekly visit from a behavioural support teacher, for one hour.

In response to this it's no surprise that the exclusion rate has
soared, or that thousands of children are truanting. The other

phenomenon is SEN children being passed around schools (we call it the Bermuda Triangle in our area – sometimes they just disappear). Parents are advised that their child is on the brink of exclusion and that this will make it harder to find another school, and faced with this pressure parents 'voluntarily' move the child. Naturally our beacon school down the road (FSM 5 per cent) is full, so any problem children won't be shifted onto them.

The impact that one disturbed child can make on a class is massive. The stress on the teachers and children can be intolerable. Jean's father has taken her out of school; we've all breathed a sigh of relief. It's only in the last few weeks without her that we've realized the difference, the quietness in the class, absence of profanities, children not bullied into making friends with her. I really do feel sorry for her, she's seen and experienced things that no 9 year old should. She badly needs psychiatric help, to be placed in an environment where she can thrive, at the moment she's a time bomb waiting to go off.

SEN coordinators spend their time not working with children but trying to monitor and control the mountain of paperwork – there're Individual Education Plans (IEPs) and Individual Behavioural Reports (IBPs) to be updated every term. We needed to get a statement for Kathy (this could mean more support in class or moving to a special school), the process is of Byzantine complexity; there's a 15-page report to fill in and then a panel hearing where they seem more interested in the paperwork (is every 'i' dotted and 't' crossed?) than the child.

Schools do buy in expert support from LEAs, all we can afford is one hour a week from a specialist teacher. Compare that with what a special school can offer – small classes, teachers with SEN expertise and well-trained classroom assistants – it just doesn't compare.

The definition of inclusion is the integration of SEN children into mainstream education. There's no single word that defines what we have today – closing special schools (many of them centres of excellence), throwing children into mainstream without adequate support, leaving them to flounder, forcing a minority of schools in 'challenging' circumstances to deal with the problems. 'Inclusion' just isn't working.

12 The Teaching Awards

Imagine you've just been mugged, some of your teeth are dislodged, there's a huge swelling over your left eye and your head is throbbing. You're recovering in the casualty ward and then your assailant sidles in and whispers into your blood-stained ear that they've entered you into a beauty competition. That could be one explanation why the government-backed Teaching Awards have not gained universal popularity among the profession. Neither are the televised finals indelibly etched (unlike *Pop Idol* or *Big Brother*) into the nation's consciousness.

Maybe in our wannabe celebrity-obsessed culture, where everyone wants to be infamous for 15 minutes, the Teaching Awards were always going to languish in obscurity. How can the story of Miss Jones, who's devoted 30 years of her life teaching autistic kids in Neasden compare or compete with that *Hello!* exclusive – 'My Divorce and Drugs Detox Hell'.

The awards began with the best of intentions, after years of 'name and shame', 'zero tolerance of failure', 'poverty is no excuse', and Ofsted inspectors trawling through schools to find Chris Woodhead's '15,000 failing teachers', they represented a brave attempt to talk up teaching and celebrate achievement. When, after two years, Lord Puttnam, the first chair of the Teaching Awards, passed the baton on to Ted Wragg, its future seemed assured. Ted was the teachers' friend, a doughty opponent of Woodhead and a fearless critic of hare-brained government 'initiatives'. And yet the awards have failed to take off, the plane is taxiing around the runway with its cargo of passengers.

Teachers *do* make a difference, we remember the complete duffers, my sister-in-law has never forgotten her geography teacher, whose lessons consisted of copying out reams of text – while he retired to tend his plants in the potting shed. But we also recall the teachers who inspired us, believed in us, lit the flame and sparked the imagination.

However, teaching is by definition a profession dominated by the team ethic. Maybe there's a suspicion of the flash individual, the attention seeker. Teachers tend to be modest by nature, hiding their light under the proverbial bushel, not wanting to shout about success from the rooftops. So what's wrong with celebrating and rewarding achievement?

The awards have also tried to reflect the diverse nature of the profession; they haven't just gone to bright young things on the promotion ladder. One of this year's regional winners for lifetime achievement was a deputy head described as the 'lynchpin' of a troubled school that had been overseen by five headteachers in two years. She was praised for her efforts to 'keep the school stable during troubled times' – a period marked by staff departures and a walkout by pupils angry at threats to discipline a teacher. She used her acceptance speech to praise the former head who left after a critical Ofsted put the school in special measures.

The winners don't all sing from the DfES song sheet. One year the secondary victor Paul Keogh attacked testing, complaining that it was damaging children's enjoyment of education. 'We are spending too much time on testing, testing, testing, and it is rubbish. My 6-year-old daughter came home in tears because she had to sit a test in silence. Why are we doing that? There is more to education than tests.'

However, the Teaching Awards have failed to capture a place in teachers' hearts.

The TA commissioned research, co-funded by the DfES, into what teachers thought about the award, they refused to reveal a full copy of the report. The best spin they could put on it was that 70 per cent of people thought it had raised the profile of teachers – hardly a ringing endorsement. They also admitted that 'those who don't engage give a more mixed response. Some misunderstand what the awards are trying to achieve. They are not into them and see them as divisive and are really quite hostile.'

One of the main criticisms of the awards is that they have been dominated by schools from the leafy suburbs – a reprise of the GCSE League Tables as the Dame Enid Latymer School for Daughters of Distressed Gentlefolk (there's always that risible quote from the head, 'we are not a selective school') powers to the top of the pile, while special measures school Gasworks Comprehensive languishes in the relegation zone.

Ted Wragg commented about the lack of nominations from schools in challenging areas and how, despite the fact that 'there is a special category for school and community involvement, which one would expect to see dominated by the thousands of inner-city teachers who make a massive contribution inside and outside the school, yet here, too, there have been relatively few nominations.'

The awards may also reinforce the 'Marvel comic' view of the world that was a feature of the early years of the Labour government – problems in the NHS – send for super-nurse; difficult class – a job for super-teacher; failing school – send for the super-head. As part of its 'zero tolerance of failure' message, the government closed schools and reopened them with new staff as Fresh Start Schools – the initiative suffered a stunning blow when in one week three of the super-heads resigned, unable to cope with the pressure. In the longer term, schools depend on teams not one or two heroic individuals.

Every survey has identified workload as the main issue that teachers complain about, yet the awards may seem to justify, legitimize or even glorify the long-hours culture. Are the winners necessarily good role models? One teacher spent two or three hours every night, and all day Sunday, on lesson preparation and marking, he also used his summer holidays to paint his classroom. There was the cautionary tale of a science teacher who left teaching altogether – three years after winning an award. She found it impossible to maintain the unreachable high standards she had set herself. The reaction to the awards from many teachers will range from a shake of the head to feelings of 'we are not worthy'.

Just as *Happy Days* was not an accurate portrayal of America in the 1950s, so the Teaching Awards jar against reality. The constant spin from the DfES seems to emanate from some parallel universe where schools are inhabited by shiny happy teachers – read the risible DfES *Teacher* magazine for confirmation of this, as ministers tour the modern equivalent of the Potemkin villages.

The most extensive survey on teacher morale was carried out by the General Teaching Council (GTC) in 2002, 70,011 teachers participated in the census. One in three expected to leave teaching within five years in protest at workload, government interference and poor pupil behaviour. More than half said their morale was lower than when they joined the profession, a third would not go into teaching if they had their time again. The longer teachers stayed in the profession the worse their morale was, with a sharp decline immediately after their first year of teaching. Eighty-six per cent said the media gave them little or no respect and 78 per cent said the same of the government.

Other surveys have shown that between a third and a half of newly qualified teachers (NQTs) leave within five years.

Despite this rate of attrition there are still many brilliant teachers who illuminate the finals of the Teaching Awards. So what are the qualities that characterize a great teacher? Passion for their subject, the ability to communicate, enthusiasm, empathy with children, sense of humour, consistency, but a key factor is confidence, confidence to take risks, change tack in a lesson – depart from the prepared script, improvise and inspire. And yet the past two decades have destroyed teachers' control and autonomy over the curriculum.

Above all there is the oppressive workload, time consumed on endless reams of paper – short-, medium- and long-term plans, every lesson planned and assessed in minute detail, boxes to be picked. Teachers are no longer to be trusted, they have become technicians rather than pedagogues.

Three years ago, the Health and Safety Executive undertook an extensive survey on stress at work. The most stressful job was teaching. This year, academics from England and Holland compared teacher stress levels across 11 European countries, measuring job satisfaction and symptoms of stress. Teachers in England were found to be considerably worst off, they scored a third higher on emotional exhaustion, and overall manifested not just more burnout but they also reported lower job satisfaction. The study established that teachers in England worked longer hours and had less personal control in their jobs. A key reason for the difference was the regime of inspections, assessments, observations and the government's obsession with grading teachers and their work.

In this era of individualism maybe teaching is one of the last bastions of collectivism and the team ethic. Possibly there's a reaction against creeping Americanization – privatization, Fresh Start Schools, fast food, WMDs. Drive down the toll roads in Florida and you'll see giant billboards with a huge smiling face beaming down at you, 'Meet Chuck Weiner – Hick County's Teacher of the Month'. No, we just don't do it like that, not yet anyway.

The Teaching Awards are struggling with the image problem that it's just for ambitious workaholic geeks from the sort of schools featured in the DfES teaching videos – rows of rosy-cheeked children in brand new uniforms, listening with rapt attention to every word their teachers utter – it's school, Jim, but not as we know it. And then there's the flakey ceremony where the finalists are slavered over by D-list celebs, New Labour luvvies and the automatons from the Teacher Training Agency – these are the people who have managed to reduce teaching to 97 'competencies'. I know some brilliant teachers who would fail on 10, and others who would pass on every one but are still as dull as ditch-water.

The Teaching Awards should be on prime-time TV with thousands of nominations from a creative, engaged teaching profession. However, against the general background of the stress-inducing workload, long hours, difficult children, the prescriptive curriculum, the fear of Ofsted and the target-driven culture of testing, the Teaching Awards will remain a lit match in a dark universe.

An edited version of this article first appeared in The Times Edu-cational Supplement.

13 The ICT lesson from hell – the barbarians at the gate

Speed and pupil engagement are two of the main advantages of the Internet. However, any new technology must be an improvement on previous practice or design. Clive Sinclair's C5 car might have looked good, but when it kept breaking down, news got around, sales plummeted.

As Broadband begins to carry all before it, many schools and LEAs still seem to be left with outdated and outmoded Internet connections. Yet again while business is using the latest high-speed technology, education is left with the equivalent of the Robin Reliant.

We went to the shiny new City Learning Centre (CLC), the Year 5 class, two students and me. The CLCs are the temples of new technology; centres of excellence – or so we are led to believe.

The lesson had been well prepared – the children paired up, more able and less able. We were ready for a fun afternoon emailing our partner school in Ireland and making a few web pages as the mood took us.

The first disappointment was the room. There is a design philosophy – cram as many computers as you can into a limited space and call it a computer suite. Jammed into a small room were 30 computers, a U-shape was cut into the rectangular room with computers all around the edges. There was no main whiteboard, smartboard or even blackboard, no focal point to teach, and not all of the children were in sight for the lesson introduction.

We started the lesson and loaded the Internet, we waited ... and waited ... and waited. After two or three minutes a page lumbered into view. We loaded the Schoolmaster site and waited ... and waited ... and waited. Another three minutes elapsed. By now some of the special needs children were getting fidgety, this wasn't helped by the swivel chairs, which were going up and down, around and around and then across the floor.

We stopped the lesson, turned off the screens (a good teaching point) and reminded everyone about our rules for ICT. Sit still, hand up, share the mouse and keyboard. We put in the name and password and waited ... and waited ... and waited. Another two or three aeons (well I exaggerate) passed by.

As the children began to write their emails, the children from the secondary school were making a racket outside, the barbarians at the gate. One of them came in and shouted across the room to one of the children. I practised the laser glare that normally reduces Year 3 to a lump of quivering jelly, not much effect there. Eventually she went out and another girl came in and shouted across, I told her we'd be reporting it to the head. They moved off outside to the next-door classroom the noise filtering in through the adjoining doors.

Meanwhile, we're still crawling through the Internet, it's like reading a book with all the pages glued together. Now I begin to understand why so many teachers don't like teaching ICT. The last few minutes I let the class go on the Tweenies site – they waited ... and waited ... and waited. Finally it was time to get the coach back to school.

Why does education always seem to get the dross? Talk about surfing the superhighway – more like stuck in a gridlock on the M6 between Stoke and Birmingham. If we were a business, we'd be sacking our ISP and getting a system that works.

When I get back to school I ring up the IT team at the council and they assure me that things will improve next week, they've been overwhelmed since the schools went back, the demand for Internet connections has increased fivefold in a month. Oh well, back to the slate and pen.

14 Christmas lights

I've always loved the *League of Gentlemen*, that *portrait noir* of a bleak, gothic, post-industrial northern town – art imitating life.

Jane and Jean had spent weeks with the school choir rehearsing all those old Christmas favourites; when the council asked them to sing at the turning on of the Christmas lights they were delighted. At this point I should explain that Blackpool Illuminations it isn't – just a few coloured bulbs strung across the shopping centre.

All week the choir had used every spare moment – breaks, assemblies – to fine-tune the performance. Jean arranged with the council for an electric generator and talked her husband into transporting the synthesizer, organ and speakers. We even had electric candles for the children to hold, risk management had ruled out the wax-burning variety.

As we trooped up to town, with our red Happy Christmas hats on, the heavens opened. It wasn't Peter Kay's fine rain; it was the unending torrential variety. Luckily when we got to the shopping centre there was a stripy canvas shelter for the choir. We managed to squeeze past the teacup ride, which looked as though it had last seen service in the Festival of Britain, and at £1 a ride was bereft of punters.

The shopping centre has seen better days; since the electronics factory shut in the 1990s people just don't have money to spend. It's full of bargain-basement shops, every day a sale day; the shops like the town are struggling to survive. There's that sure sign of distress – shops boarded up with that forlorn dirt-encrusted 'To Let' notice.

In the 'crowd' was Gemma, Year 6's ugly duckling, who was always in floods of tears when she got teased about having nits. She was really pleased to see me – a contrast to the other Year 10s, where you're lucky to get a cursory, welcoming grunt. She'd morphed into a glamorous and self-confident teenager, it made all those times I'd blasted the class for skitting worthwhile.

Dean emerged out of the gloom – shoulders hunched, hood up. One of the politest, hard-working kids; to the dismay of his parents he totally lost the plot in secondary school. He's left without any qualifications, I wish him luck – he'll need it.

The council had hired a Master of Ceremonies – with his multi-coloured coat, only the flying helmet and goggles were missing for the Roy 'Chubby' Brown lookalike competition. He held open a bag with the electric candles, the children rushed eagerly forward, 'GET BACK!' he roared. 'Don't they teach you manners in school?'

He welcomed the audience that had swollen to 15 parents and 10 disinterested bystanders. He got the name of our school wrong and was instantly corrected by the children. He mimicked their accent. Then he looked at the choir, 'Blimey, it's all girls, aren't there any lads? Oh yeah, three. The women are dominating here! Whatever you do, don't let that carry on when you get married!' We're looking at him, eyes askance – who the hell hired him?

The choir started off with 'Once in Royal David's City', mid-way through it, two trainee exhibitionists dressed as the Tweenies began prancing and cavorting, blocking the view of the choir. The arc lights picked out the rain as it lashed down on us; the narrow street seemed to concentrate the wind into a vortex.

During the second song, an elaborately padded Father Christmas made his appearance and scattered sweets into the audience, naturally he managed to miss the choir. One of Jean's felt antlers had succumbed to the deluge and was lying splattered at a crazy angle across her face, for some reason the other one was still rigid and immobile.

The town and borough mayors appeared and the MC insisted they sing along to 'White Christmas' – drowning out the choir. He then used that time-honoured tactic of every failed comedian or teacher – insulting the audience – 'I hope you get more excited when we turn the lights on, I've seen a livelier crowd in a morgue! What's wrong with you – it's Christmas!'

Out of the black sky, sheets of rain were descending on us, gutters overflowing, the cobblestones awash, torrents of water gushing down the grids. The mayors were given the order to turn on the lights, they pressed the switch – nothing. They tried again – nothing. Thankfully the three fireworks went off and scattered confetti onto the empty streets – ever since Tesco opened the shopping centre is always deserted.

We gathered the choir together, they were brilliant and in their childhood innocence loved every minute of it. When we got back to the carpark, Jane's side window had been smashed in, someone went off with her to report it to the police. I volunteered to stand guard by the car. I can still savour the moment – clothes soaked, droplets trickling down my face, frostbitten fingers, feet soaking wet, a vicious wind gnawing at my ankles, the rain turning to sleet ... such, such are the joys.

Spring

15 Reasons to be cheerful – songs to lighten the mood

It's freezing cold, the car won't start, you leave school and it's dark already. Driving rain, indoor breaks, it's that post-Christmas feeling. You're trying to lose weight, keep up with the marking and that brown envelope from Ofsted is looming. In the spirit of our times here is some uplifting music...

1. It's a Bad Day – REM
   No explanation needed.
2. Rainy Days and Mondays Always Get Me Down – The Carpenters
   Far superior to Calling Occupants of Interplanetary Craft – although I have felt like doing that some afternoons.
3. Eve of Destruction – Barry McGuire
   A great song for that pre-Ofsted period. The classic Vietnam protest song, when our school was threatened with closure I used to think of the evacuation of the American Embassy from Saigon.
4. We've Gotta Get Out of This Place – The Animals
   A hard choice between this song and the theme tune from *The Great Escape* – always a good one to whistle when you're leaving.
5. I Don't Like Mondays – The Boomtown Rats
   A song based on one of the first school gun massacres in America, when 16-year old Brenda Spencer was asked why she had shot two people, she just muttered 'I don't like Mondays. This livens up the day'.
6. Gimme Shelter – The Rolling Stones
   Not a good idea to allow Hell's Angels to steward the Altamont Pop Festival.
7. Perfect Day – Lou Reed
   How did this ever make it as an inspirational song? Supreme irony at its best, the guy's in rehab doing cold turkey wandering around Central Park.

8. I Did It My Way – Sid Vicious
   The cover version par excellence, after this it was
   downhill all the way.
9. Another Brick in the Wall – Pink Floyd
   Reminds you why you came into the profession in the
   first place – 'Teacher, leave those kids alone.'
10. Someone Saved My Life Today – Elton John
    Written after he attempted to commit suicide early on in
    his career. Surely it doesn't get that bad does it? Does it?

16 This is your flight attendant – classroom assistants as teachers

'This is your flight attendant speaking, we are currently cruising at an altitude of 10,000 feet, mid-way across the Atlantic. While your pilot is taking a short rest, I will be at the controls. If there are any problems I will notify the pilot immediately.' Result? Panic!

Under the so-called Remodelling Agreement, classroom assistants can now teach the class while teachers enjoy a two-hour break during lessons for Planning, Preparation and Administration (PPA). It might not provoke the same fear as a pilot handing over control of a passenger jet to an untrained assistant, but it's the same principle.

However, before the proverbial kneejerk reaction sets in we need to take a reality check. Every teacher knows this to be true – there are some bright, young classroom assistants that are more capable and competent than some of the cynical old lags festering in our staffrooms. Some gauche, pimply NQTs struggle to control classes that can be quelled by the stern gaze from an experienced classroom helper.

Professional elitism is a powerful factor in teaching. I well remember the car sticker, 'If you can read this, thank a teacher'. Could you find a more patronising, condescending slogan if you tried? What about support staff in schools, parents and relatives? In other professions, this approach has been kicked into the long grass. The idea that 'doctor knows best' has been tarnished forever by the scandals over children's heart surgery at Bristol and organ retention at Alder Hey.

All the teacher unions (with the honourable exception of the NUT) signed up for the Remodelling Agreement – in exchange for two hours of PPA the unions allowed the law to be changed so that instead of having a teacher at the front of the class, headteachers had the discretion to use other staff. The main beneficiaries have been primary teachers, in secondaries they have always had 'free periods', although they can be taken away to cover other lessons when teachers are off sick or on courses. This has always been a bone of contention I remember trying to urgently contact a teacher in our neighbouring secondary school: she said it had been impossible to phone on the day I rang because she had been 'teaching all day'. I think she could hear the grinding of teeth on the other end of the phone.

The idea behind using classroom assistants to teach classes was that some would receive extra training and become Higher Learning Teaching Assistants (HLTAs) and teachers would prepare the lessons. Many schools objected in principle to the idea of replacing teachers. Also schools were not given sufficient money to pay for teachers being out of class for two hours a week. At one headteachers' meeting, an official from the DfES was quizzed about how they could cover classes; he suggested inviting the local Women's Institute in to demonstrate their jam-making skills to children. I thought of some other individuals or organizations to invite –

- Equitable Life: investing your money wisely
- Stephen Byers: know your times tables
- Sainsbury's: retailing made easy
- Dan Quayle: advanced spelling
- Fathers 4 Justice: your guide to direct action
- Wayne Rooney: anger management
- Child Support Agency: computers for dummies
- Conrad Black: running a successful newspaper
- Easyjet: customer relations
- Simon Cowell: positive feedback.

Another official indulged in some 'blue-sky thinking' and pointed out that as the new legislation stipulated that there need only be one qualified teacher in a school, headteachers could dispense with the services of all of their teachers, even this was a bridge too far and he was immediately disowned. No sooner was the ink dry on the agreement and certain secondary schools began to hire people to cover classes and no prizes for guessing which Year 10 classes didn't have teachers, the GCSE revision class or the no-hopers in the SEN class. One primary school in our area gave the teachers Wednesday afternoon off and used classroom assistants to cover classes.

Eventually the lack of funding for PPA time has been so serious that the National Association for Headteachers has pulled out of the Remodelling Agreement working party. The main classroom assistants' union – Unison – voted against the agreement at its National Conference but remained on the committee.

Some classroom assistants have objected to being shoehorned into teaching classes. No surprise there, the hourly rate of pay is around £6 an hour, many receive no pay in the holidays and are on temporary contracts, every summer will usher in a crop of redundancies or reduced hours as schools try to balance budgets. The promise with the HLTAs was that the pay would go up to £19,000 a year, however there's been little sign of schools rushing to pay this. In one school, classroom assistants were told they would only qualify for the HLTA rate when they took the whole class to cover for a teacher.

If the patrician arrogance of some professions needs consigning to the dustbin of history, so does all forms of inverted snobbery or crude class levelling that destroys expertise or culture. In the aftermath of the Cultural Revolution, the Chinese attempted to solve the shortage of trained medics, through the use of so-called 'barefoot' doctors. Within months the Maoist spin-doctors claimed they were undertaking complex surgery and eradicating every disease known to man. Of course it was a disaster, in desperation many people resorted to faith healers.

In our own culture, workers in the front-line services have a healthy contempt for any substitution by under-trained and poorly paid surrogates. It would be a complete no-brainer to ask anyone in the event of catastrophic fire, serious assault or potentially fatal injury who they would want to be attended by – professional or retained fire-fighter; police officer or 'special'; trained paramedic or St John's Ambulance volunteer. On a point of principle, how can you replace a teacher who has trained for three or four years with a classroom assistant?

Classroom assistants teaching? Before some New Labour clone gives us the spin about 'freeing teachers', let us be brutally honest, in many schools faced with a dire shortage of supply teachers, they would, given the chance, throw any draconian dinner lady into 5C on a wet Friday afternoon.

That's not to say that there aren't well-qualified staff who couldn't teach lessons like PE, music or art. Why not make it easier for classroom assistants to train in school and become teachers? Thousands of them discover they have got the ability to enthuse and inspire children but they can't afford to leave work and go to college. Having another competent adult in the classroom can be brilliant, I've had exceptional people where you can virtually team-teach. Other teachers have found the burden of planning for someone untrained, badly paid and demotivated a real chore. The turnover of classroom assistants in many schools is unacceptably high.

However, the low pay and insecurity of being a classroom assistant is just par for the course. Whenever it comes to caring for people then different value systems come into play, i.e. the sick (NHS), the young (schools) and the old (care homes). The late and unlamented Conservative Education Secretary John Patten showed the real attitude of some politicians when he suggested that as nursery teachers were only just watching children play, they could save money by replacing them with a volunteer 'Mum's Army'. Faced with the wrath of thousands of nursery teachers this piece of 'blue-sky thinking' was swiftly retracted.

Classroom assistants taking classes, what does this say to aspiring teachers? How can we expect children to have any respect if the message coming from the government is that any warm body in front of the chalkboard will do?

17 Help! I'm a primary ICT coordinator – get me out of here!

It's only when you sit down and make out a list that you appreciate the enormity of the job of ICT coordinator, the everyday tasks, the technical expertise required. It's a salutary experience writing it down, just like when I moved house and had to notify 32 different organizations. As you commit memory to paper you remember this or that detail or undertaking. By the end of the process I'm empathizing with Edvard Munch's 'The Scream', or thinking of analogies with Greek mythology – the Labours of Hercules, the story of Sisyphus. The person who says ICT will save you time is a fool, a charlatan or a liar.

Over the last five years we've accumulated 16 networked computers, two printers and a scanner. A recent arrival is the Smartboard, and yes, I am an instant convert. As welcome as it is, that's another manual to read and inwardly digest, more software to master and fit into the curriculum. That's one of the main problems the sheer volume of software. On our network there are four maths programs, an English one, Granada Toolkit, Excel, PhotoEditor, PowerPoint, Publisher, Word, First Logo and the Intranet with Espresso and Spark Island. Followed by all the Internet sites to bookmark.

Then there's the Network to contend with, main tasks involve –

- adding and deleting names
- managing the shared school folder
- clearing printer queues
- installing new software
- anti-virus updates
- reporting faults.

In addition, there is the system which gives every child in the school their own email address and password. By this stage you've probably pigeonholed me as a whinging, Luddite, technophobe, but just to prove I can walk the walk and talk the talk, we've been involved in an e-pal partnership with a school in Ireland. Children have exchanged emails every week; we've sent videos and plan to video-conference.

Not only that through different bids, grants, awards and sponsorship deals, which are as much part of the educational landscape as drystone walling is to the Lake District, we've acquired a digital camera, web camera, CD writer, digital video and radio station. I've also attempted to build a school website – not helped by the LEA disabling our File Transfer Protocol for over a year.

The problem I have is the sheer scale and complexity of the job of ICT coordinator, in my five years I can count the days of training by the LEA on the fingers of one hand; for those struggling with the numeracy strategy, that's five or less. Like many other teachers I've paid for training in my own time – an MA, Joint Exam Board in ICT teaching, Internet courses. But the prevailing wisdom still seems to be, 'If we bung enough computers and software into the classroom, that's ICT sorted.'

Isolated examples of best practice by well-meaning Stakhanovites cannot hide the essential truth that training is haphazard, sporadic and unorganized. How many courses do you go on and meet the gauche NQT who has been landed with the ICT coordinator's job? When it comes to training we seem to be blighted by that dreaded word 'twilight', i.e. do it in your own time. You can always tell it's an after-school session, teachers have that Pavlovian reaction of looking at their watches, 'bloody hell, is that the time?' If you ask a question you get the death-ray glare. When are the powers that be going to grasp the nettle and pay teachers for after-school training?

Maybe we need an educational version of the First Tuesday club, where people can meet to network and swap ideas. Primary teachers tend to be isolated in their school without peer review or support. Sometimes we just need people to bounce ideas off. At the moment we're groaning under the strain of initiative overload, or ideas not planned or followed through.

Schools need to employ specialist ICT teachers just to keep up with the technology. At present we have to have knowledge of the hardware, software, networks, Internet and peripherals. Not to mention fixing basic technical faults and software pro- blems. That's before we begin to get our heads around how to actually use ICT in the curriculum!

18 Literacy planning – another disastrous training event

There are certain experiences or events that you anticipate with a mixture of dread or foreboding – that visit to the dentist; the latest Jeffrey Archer novel; another bore draw FA Cup Final between two teams of narcissistic, arrogant, over-paid mercenaries.

So last week, when the LEA summoned 100 teachers to a meeting on literacy, based on previous knowledge, my expectations weren't exactly raised. What I discovered is that there is boredom, absolute boredom and Key Stage 2 Literacy Planning Meetings. This was an hour that plumbed the depths of tedium, monotony and dreariness.

There are certain jobs that you wonder if they have any real purpose or genuine use, i.e., traffic wardens, spin-doctors, estate agents. Add to the list that quirk of evolution the literacy consultants – those cloned propagandists of the Literacy Hour, brought to you courtesy of the Raelians.

For an hour we were battered with objectives and targets, weighty tomes of Grammar for Writing, Spelling Banks and Progression in Phonics were wafted in front of us, then the final *coup de grâce*, the new planning sheets with weekly, two-weekly objectives and unit plans. When I looked round there was a sea of faces looking like trauma victims, eyes glazed, mouths gaping, eyebrows raised.

Do these people ever go into schools with the thought that they will inspire teachers? Is there a unit in the DfES that administers a frontal lobotomy for all aspiring literacy consultants?

Somewhere a Kafkaesque novel is waiting to be written about a teacher trapped in a classroom, beset by league tables, SATs and performance management, trying to teach creativity through the Literacy Hour. Or a subversive comedy called The School – the casting would be a synch, Ricky Gervais as the literacy consultant.

19 How Miss Perfect lost her smile – Briony can't quite handle my class

I've got problems with a lot of New Labour's ideas in public services. Here's one: when there are difficulties in the NHS, send for the super-nurse; failing school – parachute in a super-head; challenging class – call for super-teacher. As these supreme beings sort out the mess and save the world, us poor mortals stand back in awe and amazement.

Two years ago our LEA advertised for 20 task-force teachers. As a regular member of the escape committee, I sent for the job spec. Now, there's the scene in the film *Annie Hall* where the characters, played by Woody Allen and Diane Keaton, are having a New York-style intellectual conversation, the subtitles in the film reveal their crude thoughts. Once you read through the usual verbiage and edu-speak, it was easy to decipher the role. I mean why don't they just bluntly spell it out? 'You will go into failing schools, kick teachers up the backside and show them how it is done.'

After four rounds of local and national advertising the number of applicants was equivalent to the UK's point score in last year's Eurovision Song Contest. Our union secretary did ask the LEA if they could spend the money on something else, but no it was ring-fenced.

This academic year after some costly headhunting, three brave souls came forward. With our head's position vacant, the LEA asked if we wanted a task-force teacher until we made an appointment. To say we were unenthusiastic would be an understatement, but we didn't want to appear churlish. After all, with our abysmal SATs scores who are we to argue, we know we're all crap.

One bright Monday morning, the power-dressed School Improvement Officer appeared with Briony in tow. We mustered for a morning briefing, 'Briony's here to help, she's not here to spy, you don't have to worry...'

It wasn't an auspicious start, she spent days trawling through test results, school averages, LEA averages, national averages. One day she was in my classroom going through the DfES website on, yes you've guessed it, test results.

If that wasn't bad enough she had an irritating talent for getting on everyone's nerves – like fingernails being drawn across a chalkboard. She had that annoying habit of breaking in on other people's conversations, you name it, she'd done it, been there, got the T-shirt, seen the film, collected the memorabilia, been on the website, met the author...

Another of my pet hates are the DfES teaching videos, the ones with the perfect class, brand spanking new uniforms, rosy-cheeked, from Upper Middle Class Primary, Stockbroker-on-Thames. No one fiddling with velcro, pulling anyone's hair, nudging each other, losing pencils, twanging rulers. To mix metaphors, it's the Stepford Wives teaching the Middewich Cuckoos.

Would Briony be able to match up to this standard? Her teaching debut was awaited with anticipation. The day she'd spent in my class, they'd been excellent, yes you get days like that, no one had fallen out, it wasn't windy or snowing out-side. 'They seem a nice class', she said at the end of the day. 'Well ...' I replied.

The following morning, Briony took them for maths and English, while I went off to work on my coordinator plans. At dinnertime I came back into the class. Now I'm not Mr Tidy, but the classroom looked like a scene from Aggie and Kim's *How Clean is Your House?* – before the tidy up. A cursory glance at some of the books showed an appalling standard of work.

There was Briony, sat at my desk, slumped forward head in hands, I approached cautiously, she looked up, 'I have had the most HORRENDOUS morning. I have never known such RUDE, CHEEKY children. I want to see four of them this afternoon and I will be DEMANDING an apology.'

I was struggling to contain a grin of game-show host pro-portions by biting the corner of my mouth. 'They can be a bit ... challenging', I replied, and slunk off out of the class. By the time I got to the staffroom my hands were red raw – QCA Science Scheme of Work on Friction – rubbing the hands together will produce heat.

The other staff confirmed that her other lessons had been grade A disasters. She just couldn't cope with our children. After another week, by popular demand, she was given a free transfer back to the LEA and life returned to a semblance of normality.

An edited version of this article first appeared in the Times Educational Supplement

20 'I'm Bobby Charlton' – PE

Physical education. My generation remember that scene from the film *Kes*, Billy Casper in his borrowed (four sizes too big) kit, freezing cold hunched in the muddy goal mouth. The maniacal teacher played with such relish and abandon by Brian Glover – 'I'm Bobby Charlton'. At my grammar school we seemed to play nothing but rugby. There were two categories of players – a) the fast wiry ones who were fast enough to escape, and b) the muscular giants who inflicted physical violence. Only in later life when I took up marathon running did I really engage with sport.

That's the problem today, so few young people and adults actively participate in any physical activity whatsoever. This is often concealed by the promotion of elite sporting success, just look at the Olympics, America (the most obese nation in the world) always comes top of the medal table. A nation of couch potatoes whose only physical movement is the finger on the remote can cheer sporting success. If that's a problem you can always snaffle a few African distance runners and claim them for your own – a practice several oil-rich Middle Eastern countries have used. Either that or you're secure in the knowledge that it's probably not the best athlete that's won but the biggest drug cheat.

Premiership football clubs routinely import players rather than develop local talent, from May to August 2005 there were 139 transfers, 85 involved foreign players. Contrast that with Glenbuck, the tiny Ayrshire mining village where Bill Shankly was born, it produced a staggering 50 professional footballers.

When you holiday in Europe, you can't help but notice the modern well-equipped community sports facilities. When I was studying for my Teachers' Swimming Award we went to one of the local baths to watch the elite swimmers. It looked as though they'd been opened by Captain Webb after his heroic swim across the Channel, and judging by the peeling paint, boarded-up windows and cracked tiling they hadn't been repaired since. It reminded me of the swimming scene from *Trainspotting*. The pool was only half size, so our potential Olympians were great at speed turns but not so good at judging distances.

Of course there's always that element of choice, you can pay £40 a month for the luxury of a David Lloyd centre or Total Fitness, rather than negotiate the crumbling council facilities staffed by under-paid, demoralized extras from the *Brittas Empire*.

When you take the Year 6s to the secondary athletics festival, you really notice the difference. The children from the middle-class schools are noticeably leaner, taller, fitter and healthier; obesity is a rare occurrence. We've still got a few street fighters that can compete at football, but running and jumping is a non-starter. Also, skills like throwing and catching seem to have atrophied and died, replaced by wearing down thumbs on the Playstation. There's also the constant battle to get children to bring kit into school for lessons.

In the sporting arena the mania for success and certificates continues unabated. I briefly taught at a local swimming club, the end of the session was always marred by children striving to achieve that prized 12-metre certificate. There they were, chests heaving, red-rimmed eyes, inhaling half the pool, all under the gaze of 'competitive mum'. Then there was that inevitable question, 'Our Ashley's been going the same time as Gemma, but she's already got the 15-metre certificate.' There was a high turnover rate. When I visited a German primary school the whole emphasis of the lesson was on play, enjoyment and water confidence.

That other insidious evil is sponsorship. We had the children swimming lengths of the baths so I sent off to the Amateur Swimming Association for some certificates. When they arrived in the post, slap-bang in the middle was the grinning face of Tony the Tiger from Kellogg's Frosties (sugar content 38 per cent, second only in that league table to Sugar Puffs). Who the hell sanctioned that Faustian deal? Probably the same bright spark who got Nutella (57 per cent carbohydrates, 31 per cent fat) to sponsor a leaflet encouraging parents to help in after-school sports. Ah, so that's why so few get involved, it's not the long hours; it's all those jars of Nutella.

When it comes to after-school sport I've got to admit I'm a former serial offender, I can cite the following cases – football, girl's football, netball, cricket, swimming, judo, dance, athletics, cross country. The problem is that for many teachers, cash has reared its ugly head and many secondary schools pay their teachers. I went to one training session where the trainer admitted that most coaches wouldn't 'get out of bed' for less than £20 an hour. All we had from the LEA was a grudging offer of £8 an hour that was immediately torpedoed by the Catholic primary heads who said that under no circumstances would any of their teachers get paid. Even where £20 was offered for dance classes some governors refused to pay teachers. Maybe in this time where the market ideology is dominant, where every service has been privatized teachers have adopted the convictions and cynicism of the system – if you want it done, I want paying.

What is not understood or appreciated is the hassle and time involved: phoning schools to organize matches; getting letters out; organizing lifts; the pressure from parents about why their child was early/late/not picked. Lifts can be a major headache. At the end of one match I was facing the prospect of cramming six children in my car, one of the dads was picking up his son, I explained the situation and asked if he could take another one or two. He glowered and said 'No', then stalked off to his people carrier. Thanks pal. Go pollute the planet. On another occasion we were given the wrong venue by a local school, I had to contend with a scowling parent muttering about cock-ups and equating my organizational abilities with the preparation of a convivial gathering in a local hostelry.

Of course I miss some of the highlights; that semi-final in the netball; restraining Dominic from doing a Wayne Rooney after his goal was disallowed in the penalty shoot-out; watching Kirsty do a Roy Keane in the girl's football by nobbling the opposition.

But no, that's me done, finished, over – been there, done that. Before you write me off as a cynical old curmudgeon-like Victor Meldrew, pray, gentle reader, consider the other following mitigating circumstances: a government and media that uses every opportunity to pour excrement from a great height over the heads of teachers; the 55-hour average week; the case of our neighbouring school with excellent after-school sport. The head arrived at a reorganization meeting where, like a bolt from the blue, they were up for closure. Would the LEA help the teachers to find other jobs? Only if their consultants could observe them teaching a lesson. Yeah, thanks for all your years of service, the after-school sport, but based on one lesson with difficult children you're just a crap teacher. Needless to say the staff informed the LEA which particular orifice in the human body they could place their 'offer'.

However, if I'm brutally honest what finally ground me down was that in all those years I did it, no one ever said that simple word 'thanks'.

21 Luminous green snot – why teachers take sick leave

I'm ground down, tired, spent, worn-out, knackered. My head's pounding and I haven't slept all night. I finally admit defeat and phone in sick. I can't cope, can't face the class, not today. It just takes so much *energy* to teach 30 children, for those 22 hours (particularly with my class) you need to be at it full tilt, brain fully engaged. By the end of the school year I'm totally drained, it really does take weeks for the batteries to recharge.

I don't like taking time off, other teachers have to cover breaks. You don't want to acquire a reputation and become the school 'sick-note'. In some schools the only excuses for absence are your own impending demise, or the funeral notification from the next of kin. Supply teachers are of varying quality – another service privatized, there used to be LEA supply pools where schools could call on experienced teachers who tended to cover one school. Now, you might come back after one day to find all those pencils, rubbers and sharpeners you had been hoarding have disappeared into the ether. Or you find a desperate note from the supply detailing what a horrendous day they've had.

People taking time off are treated as malingerers; some supermarkets won't even pay for the first three days off, what do they want staff to do, infect everyone else? There's also the farcical 'back to work interview', as though you've committed a major crime, first question 'why were you off?' 'I wasn't well?' 'How unwell is that?' Of course when it comes to the City there's different standards, how often do you see people sent off on 'gardening leave'? No, the welfare of teachers seems to be way down the priority list in many schools, another disposable item that you can change like a faulty piece of machinery.

Sometimes it does pay to take time off just to show school management what you have to put up with. Our former head used to float round the school with her immaculate hair and manicured nails, you'd see her disappearing over the brow of the hill in her sports car while you were still stapling displays up. If ever there was a problem with a child, you the teacher were the problem because you weren't handling it correctly. A teacher in a neighbouring classroom was off for a week, normally our ex-head would *never* teach, but this time the supply money had run out. By the middle of the week I could hear her raised voice constantly echoing down the corridor. When it came to Friday afternoon it had risen to a screech, some children were sitting in the corridor and the classroom looked as though a nuclear device had been detonated, pencils were strewn all over the floor, bins overflowing with screwed-up paper. There she sat, hair bedraggled, nails chipped, welcome to the real world, I had to admit to the merest tinge of *schadenfreude*.

Last year, 2.7 million teaching days were lost due to sickness, however 43 per cent of staff didn't take one day off, the average was 6 days per teacher (less than the police, health workers and civil servants). Apparently it's also age related, the peak time for absences is people in their 40s, least time off is for staff in their 50s because by a process of Darwinian natural selection they are the survivors. Interestingly, scientists believe that in a post-nuclear apocalyptic future, the only animal that would survive would be the cockroach, due to its hard exterior shell, ability to scavenge for food and as a primitive life form it would not be prey to feelings of depression, anxiety and utter helplessness at the total collapse of civilization.

The long-hours' culture has become firmly established in our country (average hours per week 43.6, compared to 40.3 in the rest of Europe). Primary schools are no exception; 20 years ago the average hours worked were 44 per week, now it's 55. Ten years ago in other occupations, 10 per cent of people worked over 48 hours. That has now risen to 26 per cent, also 1 in 6 work over 60 hours. My sister worked for a mail-order company where the buyers would routinely stay until 7 pm, some of them admitted they didn't actually have any work to do, they just didn't want to be the first person to leave the car park. There's also that time-of-the-year factor, I read in the papers that 24 January is the worst day of the year. Apparently foul weather, debt, fading Christmas memories, failed resolutions and a lack of motivation conspire to depress. The formula for the day of misery reads $1/8W+(D-d)$ $3/8\times TQ$ $M\times NA$. Where W is weather, D is debt – minus the money (d) due on January's payday – and T is the time since Christmas. Q is the period since the failure to quit a bad habit, M stands for general motivational levels and NA is the need to take action and do something about it. The effects of cold, wet and dark January weather after the cosiness of Christmas, coupled with extra spending in the sales. 24 January was especially dangerous, coming a whole month after Christmas festivities. Any energy from the holiday would have worn off by the fourth week of January.

It's also the darkness and gloom that descends with the weather, one million suffer from severe symptoms of Seasonal Affective Disorder (SAD), all animals react to the changing seasons with changes in mood and behaviour, and human beings are no exception. When we had coal mines the worst shift in winter was days because you'd plunge into the bowels of the earth when it was dark, work in the total blackness of the shaft and come out of the cage into the Cimmerian darkness. Winter brings that teacher's nightmare 'wet-play', instead of letting the class out on the playground they are confined to the classroom, we always try to get them out – a veritable monsoon or deluge being the exceptions.

With my current class there are plenty of high-level disruptions – children swearing, running out of class, refusing to come in from the playground, throwing tantrums, not working in class. But it's the low-level disruptions that really grind you down, the inability to sit quietly on the carpet, interruptions, losing pencils, chatter and worst of all constantly falling out with each other.

It's not surprising that teachers take time off – try being cooped up with 30 young children who are a walking depository of every bug, germ and pestilence known and unknown to medical science. Some children have a permanent cold. I remember Duane who would stand under your feet at play time, gazing up at you with a quizzical Baldrick-like stare, he'd always have a plug of luminous green snot wedged in one of his nostrils. Then there's the annual headlice epidemic that spreads like wild fire. The constant letters home, teachers who spend all their time nit spotting, the supplies rushed in – combs, lotions, films; all to no avail, the new super-nits, the survivors, have become resistant and immune.

Those schools and LEAs with the lowest sick days are usually the ones that look after their teachers by carrying out reviews to find out why staff are absent. One survey of 350 headteachers found that over half of days off were stress-related. Some schools invest money by improving toilets or staffrooms. My own LEA seems to prefer the big stick by constantly 'improving' the sickness policy and hounding teachers who take time off. In a neighbouring LEA the staff at a secondary school voted for strike action after a teacher was absent because a pupil had assaulted her.

Coming back the next day, the classroom is still intact, the supply teacher has done all the marking but has left a note that questions in explicit terms how any normal human being could maintain any semblance of sanity with such a class. Gary has his nose pressed against the window. 'Hey sir! You should take more days off. That teacher we had yesterday was brilliant!' I tear the note up and consign it to the bin.

22 The play script – a lesson that went wrong

The literacy lesson the DfES didn't want to video

Narrator: We are in a junior school in an 'economically challenged' area. Year 5 is writing play scripts about a parent cooking tea and two children arguing about which television programme to watch. The work is going to be viewed at parents' evening. Laura has been moved to another desk – she has been talking non-stop with Sarah, she is sitting outside the classroom in the corridor, sobbing uncontrollably.

Teacher: We're going to write out this play script for 20 minutes, in quiet and no interruptions, don't put your hand up for spellings, just try it, no toilet until break time. Shhhh...

(The class begins writing in total silence. The classroom assistant goes out to try and get Laura back in, but she is still inconsolable)

(5 minutes pass)

Brian: (hand up) Can I go to the toilet?

Teacher: Break time.

(10 minutes pass by. Teacher moves James away from Ronald, the partially sighted boy who is waving his ruler around)

Brian: (Hand up, indicates he needs to sharpen his pencil)

Teacher: (Glares and indicates towards the waste bin)

(Mrs Cummings the school secretary comes in with yet another letter to parents about nits)

Brian: How do you spell 'watch'?

Teacher: Try it.

(Angela is desperate to go to the toilet; teacher points to the door, she goes out)

Brian: I've finished.

Teacher: Right, imagine the other parent comes back. What would they say? Remember to make it realistic, what would really happen?

(Angela comes back from the toilet, she's tucked her skirt in her knickers. Half the class begins to snigger. She sits back down crying silently. Teacher silences them with death-ray glares)

Brian: Eric's only written four lines.

Teacher: Will you GET ON WITH YOUR WORK.

(Classroom assistant makes final fruitless attempt to get Laura back into class)

Brian: (Hand up)

Teacher: Is it a matter of LIFE AND DEATH?

Brian: (Shakes head, puts hand down)

(Classroom assistant is frantically trying to put stickers over Brian's English book. Shows teacher the dialogue)

'**Child:** Mum, Dad's home from the pub.

Dad: Why are these kids arguing?

Mum: Fuck off.'

(Teacher collapses with hysterical laughter)

(Exit teacher, pursued by men in white coats)

23 The winding road from Ballysomething – our trip to Ireland

We're at the ferry terminal with the children; the guy with the yellow jacket and clipboard starts looking under our coach then shakes his head. Our driver starts pointing at his ticket; it appears that the coach is too heavy to go on the ramp. The driver swears he gave them details about the weight of the coach. I'm seeing months of work and preparation disappearing into thin air – we can't go back to school with our tail between our legs. I storm into the office, ready to go into an Alex Ferguson meltdown – if you're going to lose the plot with a company, do it in front of as many members of the public as possible. They hastily ring Holyhead and book us onto another ferry.

The driver makes a dash for Holyhead, but he's got to keep to 70 because of the tachograph. As we reach the outskirts of the town we can see the ferry steaming out of the port. Holyhead's business has been based around moving people through it quickly, there just ain't much to entertain a coach full of children for four hours on a wet morning. I learn that 150 years ago when it rivalled Liverpool as a port it used to have the longest breakwater in the world ... er, ... and that's about all I can remember.

Through the British Council we've linked up with an Irish school. The British Council is one of those charming old-fashioned institutions that seems to have escaped the privatization mania and is free from the obtrusive sponsorship by dubious multinationals that seems to infect so many organizations. They pay for me to go over on an initial visit. The school is right over in the west of Ireland – next stop America. The headteacher has made links with schools all over Europe and flags from different countries flutter outside the school.

Even out in the far-flung parts of the country you can see the effects of the Celtic Tiger, new buildings are springing up everywhere and families returning from Britain have boosted the school numbers. There's a brilliant EU-funded museum on an archaeological dig that shows how the climate changed and the land was transformed from woodlands and pasture into peat. There's also a darker side to Irish history, the Famine 1845–50. It's estimated that 1 million died and 1.5 million emigrated, from a population of 9 million. Every year they hold a local march to commemorate those who perished or fled.

We decide to do an email project and send film clips to each other of our children talking about their hobbies and interests. Watching the children write emails it drives me to the conclusion that men are from Mars, women are from Venus. After ten minutes, James and Michael have written 'We had a football match last week. We lost 2–1.' I encourage them to write more detail about the match, who scored, what was the pitch like, who played, where did it take place, who was the opposing team? Jean and Rachel are sending an email counselling their Irish partner who has lost her grandmother. Meanwhile the boys have made some progress, 'We had a football match last week. We lost 2–1. I scored.' The girls go on to discuss the characters in the TV soaps and a textual analysis of the different novels I have read to class. After 20 minutes the boys have finished – 'We had a football match last week. We lost 2–1. I scored. It was muddy.' The reply from their Irish counterparts is of similar brevity, except that it concerns Gaelic football.

Quite by chance I saw a Channel 4 News report, Shell announced plans to open the Corrib Sea gasfield and pipe it across the land to a processing plant close to the school. There were divided opinions within the community but Shell were stopped in their tracks by the head of the school who occupied one of the diggers for two nights (couldn't see Erica doing that) and fought them through the courts. We organized a debate in class between different groups – locals for and against and Shell and environmentalists (five local landowners are later jailed for 94 days for protesting against the pipeline).

Organizing the trip required advanced skills in logistics, the plane was too expensive and there were no flights to Knock, to catch a train we'd only have half an hour to get across Dublin, mini-buses were out because we couldn't get insurance, we finally opted for a coach and eventually find a driver mad enough to undertake the journey.

Once we get on the afternoon ferry to Dublin the children enjoy the freedom of roaming around on deck, we send out frequent patrols to make sure no one is lost overboard. We arrive in Dun Laoghaire just in time to catch the rush hour and crawl along the road out west. Years of experience teaching children has taught me that even though you may repeat a simple message many times, it will fail to register with some of them. Kevin chooses this time to turn a shade of purple . . . he's desperate for the toilet. Yes, he agrees we had told him 20 times to go on the ferry, but he'd 'forgotten'. We offer him a conveniently shaped bottle but he refuses. Eventually the driver pulls over next to some bushes and all the boys pile out – they'd all 'forgotten', the girls maintain their modesty.

It's a long drive across Ireland and we have to use every ruse to keep them occupied, I go through my repertoire of Beatles songs, much to Liam's disgust. We phone through to the Irish school to warn them we'll be late and a kindly parent volunteers to meet us in his red Cortina outside Murphy's bar in Ballysomething to guide us in. It's a good job he's in front because the road winds up and down and around, at one point there's a sheer drop down on the right to a sea loch and to the left the face of a giant black mountain. Strains of Mussorgsky's 'Night on the Bare Mountain' for woodwind quintet go through my head. I'm starting to panic, are we following the right red Cortina?

We finally arrive at 11 pm, total journey time: 17 hours. We clamber off the coach like extras from a George Romero film, the parents and children have all stayed up and there's a big banner outside to welcome us. Incredibly the boys organize an impromptu match – 'We played football. We lost 5–0. It was dark.'

The next morning we wake up at the outdoor pursuits centre which also doubles as an Irish language college. They organize some great warm-up games like making the best mummy with a toilet roll, and those fiendishly complicated jigsaws that only a Nobel prizewinner in maths could solve – that's my excuse. For many children it's their first time away from home and James gets homesick, he's into boxing and a real lad's lad, but away from his mum he becomes a quivering wreck. This serves to have a knock-on effect. We're faced with some of them wimping out on the surfboarding so we have to dole out some TLC and then the 'you're in the Marines' speech.

I decide to set an example and squeeze into a wetsuit that's two sizes too small and stagger down to the beach looking like the Creature from the Black Lagoon. The next hour I demonstrate my wind-surfing skills and show everyone how to fall off in several different positions. By the evening everyone has picked up and the children disappear into the gloom on a treasure hunt that covers miles of windswept beaches and coves; remarkably they all reappear later.

Next morning we set out in plenty of time to catch the ferry. It's a long drive and you have to marvel at the bladder control of Irish drivers because it's virtually impossible to find any toilets on the way to Dublin. We've had an unforgettable experience, some schools only manage to organize trips to the local park, we seem to have been halfway across the world but I'm getting the taste for this, next stop Africa!

24 Nothing sacks faster – the Woodhead years as advertising slogans

In English we were looking at advertising slogans – how companies use catchy titles to attract attention. At the end of the lesson I wondered how we could sum up the Woodhead years – in advertising slogans.

- Woodhead – Depresses The Parts Other Peers Cannot Reach
- Ofsted – Nothing Sacks Faster!
- Haughty Not Nice
- Ofsted ... there is a better way
- Give Blood!
- Do the Shame and Sack – and put the freshness back
- Ofsted – Raising the Standards?
- Fire! Get Out Now!
- Think Woodhead – Think Recruitment Crisis
- Stop! Look! Listen! Sack!
- Eat School, Drink School, Think School
- Woodhead's a big ... in a big world
- Call the Samaritans

25 *Hello!* – ICT awards

I'm not a regular reader of *Hello!* magazine, but whenever I visit the doctor or dentist there's always a compulsion to flick through the pages. It's invariably the same format – happy, shiny, smiling people – those risible interviews where even if the celeb has been convicted on a drug charge the week before, the searching questions will include 'Did you enjoy recording your second album?' Fortunately you are safe in the knowledge that in a few weeks' time the curse of *Hello!* will strike and the celebs will be embroiled in a vicious custody battle that will be splashed all over rival tabloids.

After reading the last issue of *The Times Educational Supplement* computer magazine *Online* with the Becta Best Practice Awards, I couldn't help thinking of this analogy. Yes, let's celebrate achievement and best practice, but when is *Online* going to comment on and reflect some of the reality at the front line? Things just aren't hunky-dory back in the waterlogged, mud-filled trenches.

Do we really need endless articles from everyone using the DfES hymnbook and singing from the same song sheet? Maybe there are other people like me who read the first two paragraphs of some articles and move on. There was a prime example last year, the piece began 'I spent all my summer holidays designing the school website ...' Sorry, but this will only appeal to a) the seriously ambitious b) dedicated anoraks c) Billy no mates d) any combination of the above.

Four years ago we began to develop our school website using AOL Press. It was only an Alastair Campbell-style 'bog-standard' site, but it was a start. Then the LEA changed the network provider and disabled our File Transfer Protocol for 18 months. After numerous letters and complaints it was restored and I had to re-learn web design. We asked for help from the CLC, their web whizkid missed two appointments to come out to school and eventually came up with a homepage that was about as much use as chocolate fireguard. Finally the classroom assistant (another disillusioned ex-teacher) at our neighbouring school sat me down for an afternoon and gave me some practical tips, i.e. how to resize images.

That brings me on to my main bone of contention – technical support, or the lack of it. After many complaints, the LEA set up a one-stop shop service – you phone us, we'll fix it. This was fine in theory, until the laptop that was attached to the white board developed a fault. The lap tops – now, that was a different company and so we had to phone them. The projector – now, that was something called a 'grey area' and we needed to phone a third company. After being passed between all three, I must admit I did lose the plot and was sent to sit in the stock cupboard to cool down.

I could go on . . . E-Learning credits. The council made a bulk purchase of Learn Premium – one of the best educational websites I've seen. Part of the package was that the LEA would give schools two days' training – ten months on we're still waiting. When we did try to use Learn Premium all the graphics froze and we could only use three computers.

In six years as an ICT coordinator, I can count the number of LEA training days on the fingers of one hand. There was one notorious session on network maintenance, it was a two-day course condensed into one, it started at 9 in the morning and finished at 6.30 in the evening. The technical manual was so complicated that apparently some teachers left in tears.

Without adequate training and decent technical support computers are like any other piece of equipment they will lie there in a corner – a point that American Larry Cuban makes forcibly in his book *Oversold and Underused* published by Harvard University Press (2002).

We also need to develop a culture where constructive criticism is valued. LEAs are always coming into schools telling us what to do, how to do it and when. Yet when we raised some reservations about ICT policies, we were told that our comments were 'unhelpful' and 'inappropriate'. But then who are we to criticize? We're just the crappy school on the scummy council estate they've tried to close down twice.

Is there any point in a few brave souls conquering Everest if the rest of the party are stuck at base camp, the ropes worn out, the compasses broken and the altimeter has been sent away to be fixed? A minority of hard-working Stakhanovites can never compensate for, gloss over or hide the painful reality. Where is the hard edge of independent, critical, journalism in *Online*? Why do so few articles reflect the everyday experiences of ordinary teachers? I just wish they'd provide more balance than the endless supply of success stories and glitzy award ceremonies, reality it ain't. Many of us are just the mushrooms – kept in the dark and fed a load of . . .

26 Ten things that are wrong with the Literacy Hour

1) Over-prescriptive

The deluge of daily, weekly, monthly plans, where every minute is accounted for has overwhelmed teachers. Where is the scope for spontaneity or invention when Letts or Ginn have done all the work for you? Good teachers adapt and adjust lessons for their class in order to account for different abilities. Teachers teach according to their own strengths and interests. However, the DfES 'guidelines' are there and it takes a brave teacher to ignore them. It's the same in foundation subjects with the curse of the QCA Schemes of Work – Ted Wragg memorably called for them to be buried in a deep trench. This year, term two, the plan was for a ten-day deconstruction (Jacques Derrida would have been proud of it) of the *Billy Goats Gruff*. After a week, I was bored and so were the children, we changed to the *Big Bad Pig* and the *Three Little Wolves*, I had the class roaring with laughter.

2) Rigid time structure

The Literacy Hour is based on 15 minutes of text work, 15 minutes of grammar, 20 minutes guided or independent work and a 10-minute plenary session. It's not an urban myth – there really were schools that bought teachers alarm clocks so that they could keep to the allotted time. The result is that children rarely engage with real books, I've used class readers where all the children have read together, the SEN children loved *Goodnight Mr Tom*.

3) Speaking and listening

The original National Curriculum contained a whole section on it – exploring, developing and explaining ideas; planning, predicting and investigating; sharing ideas, insights and opinions; reading aloud, telling and enacting stories and poems; reporting and describing events and observations; presenting to audiences, live or on tape. At the stroke of a pen, the Literacy Hour deleted this and concentrated on reading and writing, in spite of research that showed many Key Stage 1 children needed speaking and listening skills as a precursor to writing. In many schools, drama was completely marginalized or abolished. Play scripts can really engage children particularly reluctant readers who will only read for a purpose.

4) TV and film

The Literacy Hour fails to embrace or engage with TV and film, in spite of the fact that this is the dominant means of communication for children. Granted there is a danger of 'dumbing down', but you can do brilliant character studies on *The Simpsons*; with suitable editing the battle scene from *Braveheart* is great for writing about combat. The BBC's *Look and Read* produced some memorable programmes, one was about another universe connected to Earth by a wormhole, the children and I loved it, but he who must be obeyed – the literacy consultant – wasn't happy so we had to can it.

5) Guided and independent

For this 20-minute session, the class is divided into five and each group will work with a teacher once a week. The teacher will virtually ignore the rest of the class; the argument is that some teachers were 'butterflying' – moving between groups without giving consistent input to any one group. Each class is different and requires different management skills or interventions. The independent work is often boring, simple grammar tasks to keep children working 'independently'. No other country in the world teaches literacy like this, where was the research, the trials, the peer review? It never happened, another initiative written on the back of an envelope and then imposed on every school.

6) Grammar

The Literacy Strategy sets out clear goals and expectations for word and sentence-level grammar. I'm not arguing against grammar, I only learned about apostrophes ten years ago. However, you need to engage with the text first, read and write, grammar comes last, not first. The grammar targets are daunting – Year 4, Term 1 prescribes: powerful verbs, spelling strategies, verb endings, irregular tense, verb tenses, suffixes, adverbs, commas.

7) Information overload

Again, in Year 4, Term 1, there are 2 weeks on instructional writing, 1 week on reports and 3 weeks on newspapers. Whatever happened to imagination, fantasy, dreaming dreams? Some of the information texts don't exactly inspire, one was about the property of metals – great for any budding metallurgists, but when I was a kid I was interested in dinosaurs with huge teeth that ripped their victims to bits and snakes that crushed their prey into a pulp.

8) 'We don't finish anything'

Children develop as writers at varying speeds and tempos. Some need more time to write and edit. There's always the pressure to move on to the next topic, regardless of where the children are at. It's all of course based on that time-limited piece of writing for SATs, which even author Michael Morpurgo baulked at.

9) Chunks of text

Teachers and children study isolated chunks of text for 15 minutes. But only by reading and engaging with a whole book do you appreciate plot development, characters maturing and changing, the creation of tension.

10) Integration

Literacy is not integrated with the rest of the curriculum, you may be writing about Victorians in English but studying the Tudors in history. Belatedly, some schools have begun to move back to a topic-based curriculum.

The Literacy Hour was introduced during Labour's first spasm of education initiatives. Under pressure for change some schools have been given more freedom to innovate – as long as their SATs scores are good.

For those schools lower in the table there's the blanket surveillance and the dead hand of the 'consultants'. Teaching should be about using your initiative, having the freedom and the courage to innovate and experiment.

I just feel sorry for those NQTs who have never known anything else but the Literacy Hour.

27 The file of files – why paperwork is destroying teaching

We're having a staff meeting on planning and assessment, there's the green file for weekly plans, yellow for assessment, black is SEN, we put examples of children's work every term in the red English file, blue for science, grey for maths, dark green for reading records, purple for foundation subjects, there're also files of indeterminate colour for policies, coordinators, children's records and reports. Some files have evolved from binders into larger lever-arch files. When someone suggests we have a file to monitor other files, the file of files I know it's time to pack up and go home.

Planning has become the curse of teaching, that insidious blight, that ridiculous urge to record, monitor and evaluate every minute of the day. Lessons have to be planned in excruciating detail with lesson objectives made as clear as a smack in the jaw. Just to relieve us feckless teachers of that obligation and with the governments fixation of micro-managing every detail of our lives, they've produced unit plans for maths and English outlining what you should be doing in every single lesson, no need to think, it's all been done for you.

In other subjects the QCA sets out Schemes of Work for teachers to follow. Of course you can be creative and follow your own interests, but only a brave or foolish school would do that. Ofsted inspection? Falling SATs results? LEA advisors crawling all over the school? Reach for the comfort blanket of QCA. Take science as an example. When I was a kid I was fascinated about those huge carnivorous dinosaurs that could bite chunks out of cavemen – portrayed so vividly in that Hollywood film where Raquel Welch ran round in a skimpy bikini. OK, so we know from evolution and the fossil records that it didn't happen – unless you're in one of those American states where teachers are forced to inform children about intelligent design, aka Creationism.

Despite the competing influences of computer games,

children are interested in the natural environment, some of them still bring in frogs and beetles in matchboxes. But instead we cram in as many facts as possible, in Year 6 it's those simple ones to get through tests – the shorter the wire, the brighter the light, the shorter the wire, the brighter the light, the shorter the wire, the brighter the light, got it? Yeah, no wonder they're bored to tears. Here's an excerpt from the science scheme of work:

Year 3 Dissolving
Year 4 Dissolving – again
Year 5 More facts on ... dissolving
Year 6 More boring bloody stuff about salt dissolving in water

Come the revolution when teachers spontaneously rise up and throw off their shackles there will be impromptu burnings of QCA Schemes of Work, the ashes will be gathered together and blasted into space where in a few million years' time intelligent life forms will reconstruct them and marvel at the regimentation of education in an obscure corner of planet Earth.

The unit plans where every lesson is prescribed spell the death of teaching. The notion that some Whitehall bureaucrat can tell a Year 4 teacher in Grimsby what they should be doing on a Thursday morning in February is farcical. Every class is different, has distinct demands, works at a different pace, understands some concepts, and requires more time on others. The worst generals blindly, without question, follow the pre-scribed battle plan, heavy losses on the left flank? Blunder on. The unit plans for Year 5 maths had one day for percentages, one day, got it children? Move on.

The daily unit plans are there to support the Numeracy Strategy where every lesson is now prescribed in minute by minute detail. A £1m, five-year study by King's College, London, published in 2003, found that 9-year-olds who had worked with the national numeracy strategy for two years were on average only two months ahead of those taught before its introduction. The scores of the least able were actually worse.

Pupils' grasp of multiplication and division declined. And gains in National Curriculum maths tests were the result not of the strategy but of teachers teaching to the test.

New Labour's obsession with micro-managing and telling teachers what to do started from the moment they came into office in 1997. They even insulted primary teachers by instructing us to teach times tables. Steven Byers, a thrusting young education minister, was caught by an enterprising reporter, 'Mr Byers, what's 8×7?' 'Er ... um ... er ... 54?' I've had two children in my classes who knew their times tables parrot fashion, but had no idea what 13×8 was, or how to do division or knowledge of place value. The best way is to teach strategies: the 2s, 4s and 8s go together, so 2×7 is 14, double it is 28, double it again, the answer to 7×8 is 56. Learning times tables is fine, but it doesn't guarantee you'll be a good mathematician.

In teaching, you need to constantly think on your feet, adapt, amend sometimes move onto another tangent, have the confidence to depart from the script, on occasions be spontaneous. In your head you need not just Plan A but several alternatives ... what if x doesn't work? It's part of the craft of teaching that no prescribed plan or bureaucratic imposition can replace. There's also your relationship with individual children and the class. Why did integrated learning systems fail? Partly the expense but also as social animals, that dalek-speak 'well done' never could replace warm praise from another human being. Teachers need to reflect on their class: does whole-class teaching work better or group work or pairs? Planning notes should above all be a working document that can actually be used. Try teaching from the maths unit plans: you need to be either a robot faithfully reading out every question, no matter how impenetrable it is to your particular class, or to have the kind of photographic memory that can regurgitate the London phone directory.

The Literacy Hour pioneered rigid time slots, 15 minutes of word or sentence work, 15 minutes' introducing the topic, 20 minutes' independent work and a plenary or conclusion of 10 minutes. And no, it isn't an urban myth; some schools did buy alarm clocks for their teachers to stop at the allotted time.

Again, many teachers, in fear of Ofsted or hit squads coming in
to observe, have slavishly followed this formula, irrespective of
the children's needs in a particular lesson.

Trainee teachers clutch their huge planning files like a
security blanket. The Ofsted paperwork culture has infected
and crippled teacher-training colleges in a frightening way. The
expectation is that every lesson will be planned for exhaustively
and then assessed to the point of complete futility. The fact is
they never get time to *think*, reflect and actually prepare
materials to make it an interesting lesson. We had a mature
student take the Graduate Teacher Programme. They train in
schools but have to show, through incredible amounts of paper
as evidence, that they are reaching targets and expectations. In
the end our student was using a trolley to wheel her suitcase
around – she was off for a week with a shoulder strain.

The Teacher Training Agency (now renamed the Teaching
and Development Agency for Schools – another mania,
renaming things, no longer IT but Information and *Communication* Technology. Many education authorities tacked on
Lifelong Learning. Hire some consultants, change the logo, you
pays your money and you takes your choice) has a huge list of
'competencies' that prospective teachers must fulfil, from the
essential to the downright trivial. But it's all part of the mindset.
I know some teachers that would fail on 10 but are sharp,
creative and are brilliant at engaging with children, others
would pass on everything but are as dull as ditch-water.

In Finland, although teaching is not particularly well paid, it
is a sought-after profession. Teachers are educated to MA level;
they have freedom and autonomy over the curriculum. Children are taught 'altruism, self-esteem, learning how to learn,
interest in literature, maths by way of experience, creative
problem-solving, respecting others' view of life and convictions, nature conservation and respect, personal well-being,
movement and expressing oneself musically'. Compare and
contrast with the weighty tomes from the Teaching Development Agency full of targets, monitoring and planning, and then
you'll realize that the cyborgs have finally taken control. 'Come
wiv me if you want to teach.'

There are certain words that produce instant fear and

trepidation in teachers – OBSERVATION – there you are, I've said it. The Ofsted secret police strike again. That anonymous figure appears in your lesson with the clipboard; your job and the future of the school on the line, no pressure there then. It shouldn't be that way, like any other job, people starting out need help and advice. The Ofsted model is that the inspector knows best, there's a particular Ofsted-approved way of teaching and so teachers are forced to conform. Whole-class teaching is in, child-centred learning is out, topic work frowned upon, the integrated day (letting children choose from different activities) a distant memory.

Lastly, there's that other chore: assessment. Children at Year 6 are expected to reach Level 4. In the spirit of McKinsey management theory where everything can be measured, it's broken down into A, B and C stages. In many schools children are tested every year from Year 2 onwards and their progress is remorselessly tracked – spot the failing teacher. In staff meetings we spend mind-numbing hours deciding: is a 10-line essay a level 3B or 3C? The assessment madness has now transferred to other subjects like ICT and PE: what 'levels' are children at? Endless reams of paper, files, spreadsheets, graphs are wasted minutely plotting children's progress. We even had the dreaded LEA consultants in plotting English and maths targets for every term – can, will and should.

The other week there was a resounding crash emanating from the classroom, I dashed in, the shelf holding all the files had finally collapsed, dividers, plastic pockets, paper, worksheets, progress charts strewn all over the floor.

The Son of man shall send forth his angels, and they shall gather out of his kingdom all things that offend, and them which do iniquity; And shall cast them into a furnace of fire: there shall be wailing and gnashing of teeth. Then shall the righteous shine forth ... – Matthew 13.41–3

28 The leadership cult

A new headteacher has been appointed, he'll have a fair wind. I'm sure he'll be an improvement on Erica, but saying that I think any primate with basic organizational skills would be an improvement. We only had four applicants for the job, two serial candidates and two genuine ones.

Teachers aren't falling over themselves to get into management in primary schools. On average there are only 5.4 applicants for a headship. Twenty-seven per cent of schools reject all applicants and are forced to re-advertise. In the largest LEA, Kent, there are 473 primary schools, last year there were 23 schools with temporary headteachers, they couldn't find anyone to do the job, and this has now risen to 50.

I'm not a great believer in mythical 'golden ages'. If you read the *Daily Mail* this was around the 1950s – letters were delivered on time, Brylcreemed footballers didn't swear or spit, grammar schools educated our children to an amazing standard, and 'How Much is that Doggy in the Window?' was top of the charts. However, 30 or 40 years ago it was a great time to be a primary headteacher, for many it was the pinnacle of their career, a chance to innovate and play to their strengths, many schools were proclaimed for particular aspects of the curriculum – art, music, dancing, sport, writing. It was largely a male preserve (three-quarters of the workforce were female but three-quarters of headteachers were male), it's only recently that has changed. But maybe the reason so few apply for headships is that women with families choose not to work the average 50 hours per week. One third of women headteachers live on their own. The GTC carried out a survey and found that 57 per cent of teachers were unlikely to apply for any management position in the next five years.

The National College for School Leadership was opened in 2000; their training programmes contain titles like 'The

Courage of Leaders' and 'Leading from the Front'. Inspirational talks are delivered by businessmen, sports people and those self-obsessed explorers who usually manage to get themselves lost and have to be rescued at enormous expense by their back-up team. When you read accounts of these events I can't help thinking ... welcome to the cult of leadership.

It's interesting how even in business, changes have been made. I was watching a TV programme about aircraft safety, the prevailing culture was that the captain was in total control of 'their' plane. In 1977, two jumbo jets crashed into each other in Tenerife, it was the nightmare scenario and nearly 600 people died. A KLM jet was stranded in fog on the runway, waiting for clearance to take-off. The captain was receiving confusing instructions from the air-traffic controllers but decided to draw back the throttle and take-off, his plane crashed into a Pan Am plane laden with fuel. The ensuing enquiry recommended that cockpit procedures should change. Hierarchical relations were played down. More emphasis was placed on decision-making by mutual agreement. This is known in the industry as crew resource management, and is now standard training in all major airlines.

In education we have had the cult of the 'super-head', failing school – parachute in a super-head, problem solved. The so-called 'Fresh Start' approach entailed closing the school down, sacking most of the staff and appointing a new headteacher. This is another process borrowed from America – 're-constitution' – low-performing schools 'vacated' all the adults in the building, it became known as the My Lai approach – you destroy the village in order to save it.

A Fresh Start school, Firfield in Newcastle, was featured in a Channel 4 documentary in 1999. When the school was reopened, only one-third of the teachers had kept their jobs and super-head Carol McAlpine – 'I'll work 18 hours a day if I have to' – was sent in to oversee the transformation ... unfortunately it didn't quite work out like that. The programme revealed a descent into chaos; the children believed they were in a rubbish school, staff threatened to strike if badly behaved children were not removed, and attendance figures were massaged. Within a year, Carol McAlpine had resigned, followed in the same week by three other super-heads. The Fresh Start scheme was quietly sidelined.

The fear of failing an Ofsted inspection is a powerful force inhibiting teachers from becoming heads. It's seen as a personal failure, there's the football manager syndrome – poor results, sack the headteacher. The job has become more administrative, managerial and accountancy based, heads teach an average of 3 hours per week, but that covers small rural schools where they may teach half the time through to large urban schools where they may never or very rarely teach. When I visited Germany, the head in a two-form entry school had seven hours for administration and spent the rest of the time teaching. She was part of the teaching team, first among equals, and there was a far more collegiate approach to running the school.

LEAs also place impossible demands on headteachers, SATs targets are often imposed from above. There is blanket surveillance by LEA officers. Within a few weeks of our head's appointment the School Improvement Officer (interesting use of language, we used to have 'Advisers', how is improvement used? 'There must be a big improvement in Jean/John's work next year') was in for a day, swiftly followed by the literacy and numeracy consultants. Schools tend to vie against each other, share expertise and resources? You must be jesting; they're our rivals. With schools closing it's a dog-eat-dog world, we're all competing for those precious commodities called children. At one of the local heads' meetings the LEA offered £5,000 to any school that wanted to apply. Apparently it was like a feeding frenzy, jackals fighting over a bone, heads dissing other schools in the frantic scramble for scarce resources.

Headteachers can become remote from their staff, but that is often the accepted and preferred model. Not being able to confide in or trust other people is a significant contributor to stress. In 2000 the National Association of Headteachers conducted a survey of 300 members in Warwickshire – one in four reported serious health problems including high blood pressure, chronic insomnia and eating disorders; half claimed their families' lives had suffered; and one in six said they were alcoholics.

Burnout is a common reason for headteachers leaving. In

2000 Kevin Short, the brother of Labour politician Clare Short, resigned from Hamp junior school, the most socially deprived in Somerset, 'The battle has consumed my life for the last five years and it's brick-wall stuff. I've just turned 52 and I'm getting weighed down by it.' SATs pass rates soared from 18 per cent to 46 per cent but it meant working 70 hours a week, 'you have so many initiatives pouring in from everywhere, but there's no conduit to control how much arrives ... We need to spend time dealing with low expectations, lack of role models, feelings of inadequacy and not just thinking: right, we're going to do some more English or grammar, or maths.'

One of the most depressing columns in *The Times Educational Supplement* is 'How I turned the school around' – a new head in a failing school. It's true in some cases it has been through music, art, sport and creativity but it usually follows a set pattern – a SATs boot camp is introduced, results soar (reading between the lines you know that Year 6 will have endured constant revision and testing), half of the staff have been sacked and the rest have been terrorized into submission by constant lesson observation and assessment. The new head always aims to move on after two or three years with another notch on their CV belt.

The latest pronouncement from Ofsted is that they want to see 'continual improvement' every year in each and every school. I wonder if this model applies to business? What about M&S, Sainsbury's, Rentokil, etc.? In truth schools, like other organizations, regenerate, change, stand still, leap forward, tread water, retreat or even decline. There may be pressing external factors (schools in mining areas suffered alongside the communities), or particular internal determinants – a school may lose irreplaceable experienced staff who have built relationships with children over many years and gauche NQTs may struggle to cope with challenging classes. On the other hand a bunch of cynical old lags stagger into retirement and are replaced by bright energetic young teachers who transform the whole atmosphere in the school.

I don't want to minimize or downplay the role of leadership, it is crucial to the success of any school, and I know from personal experience the price of the absence of leadership. In primary schools, headteachers have to operate within the straitjacket of SATs and league tables. In our LEA you would have to acknowledge their consistent monotheism because there is only one God – exam results.

There are still heartening stories out there of headteachers who have transformed their school and the lives of the children. David Wrinkley's book *Handsworth Revolution* (published by Giles de la Mare, 2002) is really inspiring. He had confidence in his teachers, allowed them the space to innovate and above all he involved the community in the school. Being a headteacher these days is a high-wire act – there's no safety net if you fall.

Great headteachers are remembered forever. My father was educated by Greening Lamborn at East Oxford Primary School. He inculcated in children a love of poetry and painting, he also had some of the highest pass rates for the 11-plus. My father won a scholarship to the city grammar school but his parents couldn't afford the school uniform (my grandfather was dying of TB). The story has been passed down the generations how Greening Lamborn went round to the house and begged his parents to let him go.

I read in the papers about a headteacher who also used poetry, music and art to revive a failing school, he also improved the SATs results and was invited by the Department for Education to an award ceremony at a swanky London hotel. He accepted the gong and then in front of the assembled dignitaries and media scribes launched an all-out assault on Ofsted, SATs, league tables – how all this was destroying education and they could stuff their award. . . . I think I'd have done the same.

Summer

29 Stressbusters – an unusual staff meeting

Some of the local headteachers (not exactly famous for their concern about the health and welfare of their staff) are worried about stress. Under pressure with planning overload, maths and literacy coordinators are falling like flies and going off on long-term sick. With Ofsted inspections impending some heads are feeling the strain as well.

In time-honoured fashion the Local Education Authority has responded by sub-contracting the problem out to a team of 'consultants' – stressbusters. They organize a session after school in lieu of a staff meeting. We decide to meet in the more intimate surroundings of the nursery.

Our smiley trainer explains that stress is BAD, she will show us some exercises and chill-out activities to combat it. Already I'm thinking cause–effect, maybe there are other alternatives like less paperwork, cutting hours, scrapping Ofsted...

We start with an 'ice-breaker'. As soon as that word is mentioned, people freeze. It's that part of the brain that stores memories, memories of other training sessions where you have to form a circle, hold hands, hum and find your inner self. Of course, being British touching other adults is anathema to us. Thankfully it just involves throwing a ball to each other.

The trainer introduces a second ball and we have to shout the person's name that we are throwing to. I liven it up by throwing it to the wrong person, the balls scoot under the benches, sandpits and tanks full of wriggly tadpoles. I can see that the trainer has identified me as a possible malign influence on the group.

Next up is the cuddly toy, we have to pass it around the circle and say something 'nice' about the person we are handing it on to. My Sheer Utter Futility System begins to send out warning signals. Some of the staff pass on this.

Sensing our bemusement she moves on to the relaxation session. The smell of Tuscan rose hip wafts across the room from an aromatherapy saucer, mingling fragrantly with those other nursery smells of sweaty socks, Playdough and those unmentionable things that young children do.

We are encouraged to lie back on the gym mats. Looking out of the window I can see some of the children peering through the metal fence outside, wondering in awe, faces pressed in the gap distorted like goldfish.

We lie down obediently on the grimy, dirty, frayed mats. I'm not really in the mood to relax not after a day in front of my class; I need an extra-strength lager or a shot of absinthe. I hear a tape go in the cassette player and gentle panpipe music drifts across the room, the sort you hear in hotel lifts or when the dentist is just about to drill into your jawbone, my bottom lip begins to tremble.

After a minute or so 'the voice' begins to explain about relaxation, she will take us to another place. It's the sort of dusky, dulcet Home Counties voice you hear on Classic FM, reading out requests for Beethoven's 'Ode to Joy' from implausibly happy family groups stuck in a horrendous traffic jam on the M25, on their way to some cheesy kith and kin reunion. That's when I begin to lose control of the entire lower jaw.

'Imagine you are walking through a grassy meadow, the sun is shining on your back, you can feel the warm gentle wind through your hair, the small of cut grass lingers in the air. The sound of the lark wanders over into your ear . . .' By now I'm going into spasms, my shoulders are shaking, left hand clamped on my nose, snot filling the nasal cavity waiting to explode on my face.

At this point the trainer whispers in my ear, 'Do you need to go outside to compose yourself?' I make a dart for the door, fumbling to open it, closing it as gently as possible. Collapsing, back against the door, tears streaming down my face, chest heaving.

Stressbusters? I haven't laughed so much for ages.

30 'A quiet rural location' – what the adverts really mean

You've all heard the estate agents' jargon, i.e. 'in need of some repair' means 'falling to bits'.

Here is the bluffer's guide to those job descriptions about teachers and schools.

Job Description	Reality
Idyllic rural location	Miles from anywhere
The Ofsted Report highlighted many strengths...	Whatever you do, don't read the **whole** report
High parental involvement	You can never get rid of them after school
Children sometimes display challenging behaviour	The kids are out of control
We have a strict discipline code	See above
Dynamic, innovative and creative teacher wanted	The head's a slave driver
Must be resourceful and independent	You'll never see the head
Stable group of staff	They're all over 50 and can't wait to retire
NQTs welcome	We've got no money
Improving school	Failed Ofsted
Child-centred school	No longer applies
Expanding school	Huge classes
Must have good interpersonal skills	The last teacher was hated by all the staff
...would be an advantage	...absolutely essential
Good sense of humour an advantage	The head's mad

Must have good organizational skills	You'll be filling in forms every night
Experienced teacher required	We've had a load of NQTs who couldn't hack it
Challenging inner-city school	Fort Apache – the Bronx

An edited version of this article first appeared in The Times Educational Supplement.

31 A consultant calls – someone else who can't hack my class

In medicine a consultant is a doctor who has taken years to train in a particular specialism. In education they seem to be the problem, not the cure. Beware! Poor SATs results will result in a severe case of 'consultantivitis' – a potentially life-threatening disease where normally sane people begin to talk gibberish and consult graphs and tables.

We had one consultant who resolutely refused to teach our classes, he'd only observe and criticize. At least Eric was prepared to take the plunge, I was there to watch the English lesson. To say the class is lively is a euphemism – bloody hard work more like it.

Call me old-fashioned, but with any new class you need to lay down some ground rules and it helps if you talk to their previous teacher. Eric plunged straight in – within a few minutes he'd lost them, Fred was falling asleep – watching too many late-night videos, Jean couldn't concentrate, she'd hadn't had any breakfast – Mum had forgotten the Methadone prescription, he sailed on oblivious.

The introduction lasted too long, he was over-familiar and they began to take liberties – even my death-ray glare wasn't working. The good ship 'Literacy Hour' was holed below the waterline, listing to stern and a few passengers had been lost overboard. As the lesson progressed it slid remorselessly to the bottom of the ocean, the occasional bubble breaking through to the surface.

When I looked at the children's work, most of it was rubbish, the lesson focus was on sci-fi, Dean had got confused and written his usual story about a bear in the jungle. I couldn't help feel a touch of *schadenfreude*.

Worse was to come – the staff meeting was on target setting, there were reams of paper full of edu-speak, incomprehensible jargon and the bleeding obvious. 'To help raise standards give out homework and use oral feedback during lessons.' I could feel an involuntary hand motion, the fingers drumming on my cheek – mental note – next time I see Darren not using full stops I must tell him. DURRRHHH!! Like we're all a useless bunch of Klutzes.

Targets for every half-term were revealed, the class divided into three – will, must and can. Said targets to be prominently displayed in classrooms – blimey, that'll be miles better than the one I did on bats. Only the thought of the surreal kept me going – maybe I could 'challenge' the top group to win the Carnegie Prize.

By now I was at one with the Guantanamo Bay hostage who was waiting for Jeremy Beadle to come in. Finally Eric had to collect half the sheets in because he'd got the targets in the wrong boxes. There was only one solution as Ned Seagoon said, 'Burn it, memorize the ashes and eat the remains.' No, on second thoughts the recycling van was coming round the next day.

32 Let them eat marrow – school dinners

It says something about our celebrity culture. For years charities have produced worthy reports, unions protested, MPs spoken in the House, yet it took a celebrity chef before everyone woke up to the appalling state of school dinners and the government was forced to act. Strange how target-obsessed New Labour who are 'tough' on every standard failed to spot that their chums in business were serving offal to school children.

I'm not attacking Jamie Oliver, it took courage to take on the catering multinationals – the guy needs beatifying. The problem is that, since the TV series, numbers taking school meals have fallen by 15 per cent. In many areas of the country the situation is dire, 17 LEAs provide no hot meals whatsoever, and new schools are being built without kitchens.

Somehow the scandal over school meals exemplifies the attitude in our get-rich-quick society towards children. In 1980 the Tories scrapped the strict dietary rules (fat, sugar and salt content) that applied to school meals; this prepared the way for compulsory competitive tendering in 1986. You don't need to be a genius to work out that the LEAs would struggle to rival Slurry & Co with their reheated burgers 'n' chips supplied by staff on poverty wages.

The BBC made a documentary using hidden cameras about the appalling standard of care in many private nurseries. Poorly paid, under-trained teenagers were seen smoking, gabbing away and generally ignoring their charges. Contrast this with Denmark where people with university degrees undertake childcare. So when it comes to school dinners we end up with reheated, reconstituted offal – average price 37p.

Eager to spot an opportunity for profit, firms like Scolarest (owned by catering giant Compass) moved in to scoop up contracts. Using economies of scale they have been able to achieve huge cost savings, but it has become a race to the bottom. Also under the new Public Finance Initiative (PFI) schools have signed long-term 25-year deals with private companies. Who supplies the meals? In Merton the schools are managed by a company called New Schools, they sub-contracted all services to Atkins Asset Management, who in turn sub-contracted school meals to Scolarest. Some 450 other PFI schools are tied in to long-term contracts of this nature.

Privatization, cost cutting, disregard for safety, complacency in high places led directly to the Hatfield rail crash. In the years after hospital cleaning was privatized, the number of cleaners fell from 100,000 to 55,000. Our public services that used to be an example to the rest of the world have fallen into disrepair, picked to pieces by the corporate vultures.

Of course there is the danger of gilding the lily – there never was a 'golden age' of school meals, it was more bangers 'n' mash and spotted dick than Mediterranean cuisine, albeit that it was cooked on site. The other consequence of privatization is that school catering staff have become de-skilled. There's a compelling scene in the film *Super Size Me* when they visit schools in America – meals are provided by cost-cutting multinationals. The film crew go into the kitchen and virtually everything is processed high-fat convenience food, reheated from the freezer. When services are contracted out further savings are made because staff lose pensions, sick pay, holiday entitlements – another reason why people become demoralized and demotivated.

Once the standard of public services becomes so abysmal the better off opt out or pay for something better. Only 30 per cent of children pay for school meals, so the reasoning becomes if it's for the poor – save the taxpayer. We've been here before, in 1832 the New Poor Law legislated for the building of the grim workhouses, poverty was viewed as a crime and the diet of bread and gruel was meant as a deterrent. The overseers were notorious for cutting corners and buying the cheapest food to save the ratepayers any expense. In one infamous case at Andover in 1845, inmates who were given the menial job of crushing bones were so hungry they were fighting over the marrow to augment their meagre diet.

Go round the school hall at dinner time and the packed lunches are no better than the fare from the kitchen – crisps, chocolate bars, sugary drinks, yoghurt, white bread – as though some diabolical, malevolent evil gremlin is condemning children to a future of diabetes, heart trouble, piles and tooth decay. Scientists predict that, on current trends, half of children will be obese by 2020.

Children's diets are so laden with sugar that fruit and vegetables are YUK! There was a scene in *Jamie's School Dinners* when he was so frustrated with children baulking at fresh food that he got a chicken, cut out all the parts used in chicken nuggets (skin, fat, gristle), put it in a blender and showed children the grisly results. This clip should be buried and preserved in time capsules so that future generations can see how children in this age were abused and neglected.

33 Looking down the barrel of a shotgun – our school gets inspected

We've survived! A week gazing down the barrel of a shotgun – the dreaded Ofsted inspection. There's usually a 'dip' after Ofsted as teachers' nerves recover, an intake of breath, a spate of sickness, staff waiting for the next holiday. To me it feels like we've been defiled as though a total stranger is judging the most intimate of human experiences. You are observed in the different stages of sexual congress, where the penalty for failure is imminent castration (to continue the analogy with Ofsted, the inspectors have not taught for many years) and the person sitting in judgement with the clipboard is a long-term celibate.

How did it ever come to this? Her Majesty's Inspectorate of Schools (HMI) was established in the nineteenth century, the poet Matthew Arnold was Chief Inspector between 1851 and 1888, he was instrumental in the abolition of Payment by Results. Through most of the twentieth century, HMI was one of those peculiarly quiet, unobtrusive, quintessentially English organizations that nevertheless had a huge influence in its chosen field – think Radio 3, the Women's Institute, the WRVS. All sides – teachers, LEAs and government – respected HMI. Its inspectors regularly visited the schools they were responsible for.

A modern feature is the run-down of public services, the identification of failure and then the subsequent privatization. During the 1970s, the number of inspectors fell from 500 to 350, by 1983 there were only 260 left and schools were rarely visited. In 1992 the Office for Standards in Education (Ofsted) was established to inspect schools. Its first Chief Inspector was Chris Woodhead, an archetypal poacher-turned-gamekeeper, former progressive, who with the zealotry of a convert, was transformed into a latter-day bounty hunter trawling schools for '15,000 incompetent teachers'.

He was assisted by an ideological campaign that was popularized by the press – falling standards; feckless teachers and failing schools. All this was designed to erode public confidence in education. It's a no-win situation – poor SATs results at 11 means 20 per cent of children are thick; record GCSE and A level results – exams are dumbed down, too easy.

Ofsted's remit was to visit schools every 6 years (shorter inspections are now meant to take place every 3 years) and produce a public report. Schools are graded, with the worst identified as having 'Serious Weaknesses', and the ultimate hell, 'Special Measures' (they may have abolished public execution in 1868 but Ofsted reinvented it). This means that a team of inspectors visits every term until the school receives a clean bill of health – one school stayed in special measures for ten years! The worst aspect has been the twist of the media's knife, headlines such as 'School for Dummies' and 'Is This The Worst School in England?' The stigma can last for years, children believe they must be useless and so are the teachers and their school.

The House of Commons Education Select Committee noted recently that failure could send schools into a spiral of decline. Some 43 schools judged to have been in serious weakness in 2001/2 had declined further and were placed in special measures the following year. They noted that schools were 'unable to attract high-achieving pupils or well-qualified staff, making improvement more difficult'.

Every survey or study has also shown that most schools in difficulties have abnormally high numbers of children receiving FSM – the most common indicator of social need. Research by Ruth Lupton of the Centre of Analysis of Social Exclusion at the London School of Economics found that out of 180 schools deemed to be failing in 1999/2000, 90 per cent were in less advantaged areas.

Another problem is the 'falling off the cliffs' scenario, where schools only ever get help or advice when there is catastrophic failure. The Ofsted inspectors take a snapshot, visit and never return, someone else has to pick up the pieces.

Teams of self-employed inspectors bid for work, often the lowest bidder will win. The teams tend to vary widely in quality and competence. One team was found repeating whole chunks from another school's report. In another case, a headteacher whose school had failed an inspection became ... an Ofsted inspector. I wonder what type of mind set it takes to be an Ofsted inspector, but then if the post of state executioner was resurrected I'm sure there would be a flood of applicants. A part-time job on £40,000 a year, stay in a nice hotel and strut round a school looking important (snoopers, voyeurs and sadists welcome to apply), what could be more agreeable?

Before the inspection headteachers have to fill in a mind-boggling long form known as the 'SEF' – self-evaluation form. It details just about everything in the school. It's there to catch headteachers out, admit to a weakness and they'll pounce on it, leave it out and they'll want to know why. Inspections are unbearable for headteachers; failure is a comment on their life's work and will automatically lead to dismissal – unless they are comparatively new to the school.

Inspections are built around 20-minute observations of lessons. Now a bad lesson is a bad lesson is a bad lesson. The children may be out of control, the teacher shows poor subject knowledge, the explanation is unclear, work may be too easy or too difficult, the pupils learn very little. Similarly, a play may have a ludicrous plot, the acting is atrocious, the lighting and acoustics poor. But everything else is a matter of opinion, people see the same play but have differing viewpoints.

Ofsted inspections concentrate on and highlight failure. It is like a criminal trial where there is no counsel for the defence, and the best hope is for a grudging acquittal. Like a malignant cancer Ofsted has burrowed into the bloodstream and infected every organ. Teachers don't take risks, dull uniformity has become the practice, teach the standard Ofsted lesson, mediocrity has triumphed.

During our previous inspection we managed to pull the wool over the eyes of the inspectors. Policies? We borrowed them from other schools and stuck our name on the front. For once our [former] head was fully engaged – in survival mode. We scraped through, but we knew that with our poor SATs results it wouldn't be so easy next time. In the weeks before the inspection the staff stayed until late, came in at weekends. Not me, I wasn't going to justify myself by having a nervous breakdown for a bunch of has-beens and refugees from teaching.

Our Registered Inspector (the team leader) was all hail-fellow-well-met. But we knew he was the smiling assassin – in his last inspection he'd put a school into special measures. He revealed that when he looked at our SATs, that was our intended fate. The other inspector was stern and unsmiling, about as much human empathy as Rosa Klebb, the stereotypical 'baddie' in the James Bond film *From Russia with Love*.

The worst part of an inspection is the tension and uncertainty, you just don't know when they are going to come in, will it be *that* moment when the lesson goes pear-shaped? Will it be the time when one of the children decides to kick-off? Hail-fellow-well-met appeared in my maths lesson, I knew that would be a focus given our poor test results. I'd differentiated the work, the top group was working on higher multiplication, at the end of the lesson he said I hadn't challenged them enough, I knew he wanted to find fault. However, he gave it a 'satisfactory'. You might think that would be fine, but in the bizarre world of Ofsted, if too many lessons are just 'satisfactory' the school will fail. I decided not to argue the toss with him, the mind was already set.

After the first two days of an inspection you usually predict the eventual result, no lessons had failed and the children were on their best behaviour. My PE lesson got rained off and I had to hold it in the hall – always have Plans B and C. I got children to demonstrate and evaluate each other, to my relief it passed with a 'good'. The ICT lesson on spreadsheets went well – my subject and English passed with a grudging 'good' from Rosa Klebb, although I think it really hurt. Often it is just luck, I prepared a brilliant geography lesson about land seizures in India, different groups acting and debating points of view, it turned out to be an absolute disaster, the children just didn't work well in the groups, luckily they didn't watch it. Overall, 75 per cent of the teaching in the school was deemed to be good or better.

In a system that depends on people working together inspections are divisive, different year groups are singled out for praise or criticism, individual lessons are pulled to pieces, particular teachers singled out. In my friend's school, teachers who didn't really contribute to the school pulled out all the stops for

Ofsted, books that were never marked sprouted red ink markings and were showered with stickers. Who had the largest smiles at the end of the inspection?

Every aspect of the school is graded, the top being a '1'. Playtime is one of our main problem areas and we've tried everything, more lunch-time helpers, play leaders, toys, redesigning the play area, calm areas, trees planted . . . but on some days it's still a war zone. To get a '1' for playtime you need a 'calm peaceful atmosphere'; the only way we'd ever get that is to lobotomize one third of the children. By contrast, one of our ex-teachers where they hadn't done anything about playtime got a '1' in her new school, the worst incident in a term was one child getting called 'thick'.

The best way to survive an Ofsted inspection is to accentuate the positive aspects of your school, if there are weaknesses then you're aware of them and have a plan to deal with them. Above all be prepared to stand up to them, show you won't be a doormat. Mike Kent, headteacher and *TES* columnist, took Ofsted on and appealed all the way to an independent ombudsman over an unfair inspection report – and won.

One of the worst aspects of teaching is the way that Ofsted have insinuated their prescripts into teachers' lives, into the very core of the way they teach – the academic term is 'colonization'. In a dictatorship people's everyday life becomes haunted by the regime, it even intrudes into their personal life, the family dining table and casual conversation.

There's no denying that we need accountability for public institutions. A powerful argument is that 'producer capture' of these organizations effectively ignores the rights of the consumers. Schools have not always welcomed and involved parents, hospital consultants have an interest in extending waiting lists and many council tenants hate the way they are treated at housing offices. However, there must be a better way than Ofsted inspections, an expensive, adversarial, confrontational system that has produced a climate of fear, demoralized thousands of teachers and selected its victims from already fractured communities – how many schools in the leafy suburbs ever fail? Schools in crisis need continual help, advice and support, not a hit squad that periodically descends on them.

Many of them lack the internal resources to effect change – an effective group of school governors, committed parents and well-motivated children.

Even though 75 per cent of our teaching was 'good or better', we escaped serious weaknesses by 'the skin of our teeth'. The staff went down the pub to celebrate; I didn't join them, I was raging. Teachers in the face of the Ofsted onslaught become like the traumatized survivors of domestic violence, 'we did deserve it didn't we?' After years of teaching, we survive being labelled as moderately crap by the skin of our teeth. No offence, but there are good teachers in nice schools in the leafy suburbs who wouldn't survive 5 minutes in front of some of our classes.

There's that knowledge, as well that unless the SATs results improve, special measures beckons the next time round, we're still in the condemned cells – dead men on borrowed time.

34 The Heart of Darkness – the problem with SATs

This is a journey into the Heart of Darkness. Testing, that rancid, malignant, cancerous tumour that spews forth its toxins into the bloodstream; that evil Tower of Babel that casts its dark shadow over us all; that insidious pollutant that seeps into every pore. Testing, SATs and their evil spawn the league tables have been the enemy of creativity, distorted learning, choked initiative and drained our energy. We all feel their presence lurking behind us like malevolent phantoms.

Whither Year 6? What used to be the best year in primary schools has become a drudge. Children on the cusp of adolescence, just before Kevinitis sets in, and they become as communicative as Beagle 2; it used to be a pleasure to teach them. Now Year 6 is the poisoned chalice, all volunteers take a step backwards.

Year 6 is a year of revision, tests, tests and more tests. Children live that year in the shadow of the exams in May. Parents worry about the levels of stress – manifested by their children's behaviour. For teachers it's the Labour of Sisyphus, pushing the boulder up to the top of the hill, only to watch it slide down the slope when the school year begins again in September. The league tables are a public auto-da-fé as schools are pressured from all quarters. Crude comparisons are made between different schools – like organizing a race between a Formula One racing car and a battered Ford Escort, then berating the losing driver for their failure to compete.

In school, Year 6 seem to go into some kind of purdah, reduced to invisibility, it's as though they've been stolen by the Gobblers and temporarily inhabit a parallel universe. In many schools extra-curricular activities are suspended and a cultural Dark Age descends on pupils. Most pupils hate and detest the exam week, a time of stress, fear and loathing – welcome to the new millennium.

At the end of the tests teachers 'hit the wall'. It's that long haul until July, that feeling of running on empty. And then they say, be creative, innovate – like telling someone to be a celebrity cook in a famine zone.

We really need a renaissance for Year 6. In the true meaning of the Chinese proverb, 'Let a Hundred Flowers Bloom'. I'm not saying it's going to be a spontaneous uprising, like that moment when the pupils tear up the turgid textbooks in that schmaltzy Robin Williams film *Dead Poets Society*, but the fact is we need an end to the testing and league tables regime.

We need to give parents an alternative vision of what Year 6 could be like. Children should get the chance to –

- learn a foreign language
- improve the link with secondary schools for Year 7
- write a short story
- learn to play a musical instrument
- go on an adventure holiday
- put on a play
- undertake a community project.

During the sunset days of the Soviet Union, targets had become so completely and utterly discredited that no one believed, trusted in or relied on them. Everyone knew they were a fraud, a conceit and a lie. Yet because jobs and careers depended on them, people struggled to achieve the target.

The problem was that every artifice and dodge was used to realize them. One year the nail factories were given targets based on quantity; so they churned out millions of microscopic 'nails'. Most of the production had to be scrapped and there was a shortage of nails. The target was subsequently changed to one based on the weight of nails produced. Factories then churned out thousands of huge nails and the target was again exceeded.

Teachers', heads', advisors' and ministerial careers are made or broken by fulfilling the targets. But if ever there was a time to shout 'The Emperor has no clothes', this is it. In primary schools it is well documented how testing has led to teachers teaching to test; Year 6 becoming an unremitting grind of endless revision; the narrowing of the curriculum and the orchestration and manipulation of exams where every ruse and strategy is used to make the target.

There's the hierarchy of pressure – bigger fleas on smaller fleas. It starts with the government who put pressure on the LEAs, in turn they squeeze the headteachers, then the thumbscrews come out for the teachers, who in turn cajole, chivvy and browbeat the children.

Testing has entered the school's lexicon, as SATs time approaches, children become a secure Level 4, or he's a borderline 3/4, or she'll only make a 3. Schools place impossible burdens on children as revision begins earlier and earlier, art, music, history are jettisoned and that final misnomer 'booster classes' after school and at weekends. It's a bit like the argument for corporal punishment; we're bound to get traumatized survivors reassuring us 'It never did me any harm.'

To reach the target you teach to test months before, force-feeding them gruel and more gruel. Remembering that the key group to work on is the borderline group; special needs – forget them they'll never get there; the brighter ones – they're already there, let them get on with it. No, spend the teaching time coaching that fraction of the class that will be the difference between success and abject failure. If you fall short there's always that guaranteed sure-fire alternative – CHEATING. A few figures changed, those stray decimal points, that empty answer box.

There are many cases where teachers or headteachers have succumbed to the temptation and altered the odd answer or even systematically cheated. In 2002, Cynthia Thumwood resigned as headteacher of Hanover Primary school in Islington. Cheating allegations were brushed under the carpet for a year by the private firm that ran education in the London borough of Islington. A dossier of concerns compiled by teachers at Hanover Primary was passed to Vincent McDonnell, then head of Cambridge Education Associates Islington.

The document alleged that Cynthia Thumwood had tampered with maths papers for 11 year olds. But CEA, which won the £15 million, seven-year contract to run Islington's schools in 1999, appeared to do nothing with the information. Hanover came third in the LEA's league table that year. During the next tests in May 2001, further allegations by staff prompted the company to contact the QCA, the government's exams watchdog. Investigations by the QCA and CEA were carried out, but their findings were not made public. The QCA probe led to Hanover's results in English, maths and science being annulled. As a result, the school came bottom of the national league table.

Cynthia Thumwood left in December 2001, eight months before she was due to retire. No action was brought against her, or any other member of staff. In 2002, results at the school dropped dramatically. The proportion of 11 year olds reaching expected levels plummeted in comparison with previously published figures. In maths, the Level 4 total fell from above 95 per cent – consistently one of the best in the borough – to around 68 per cent.

In 2004, a Kent headteacher who was jailed for forging more than 140 examination papers was banned from teaching for life by the General Teaching Council of England. Alan Mercer, 47, was given a three-month prison sentence at Maidstone crown court after pleading guilty to changing answers on his pupils' test papers. He admitted altering and adding answers to papers over two years while he was headteacher at South Borough primary in Maidstone, Kent, in 2002, and at Eythorne Elvington primary in Dover, between 2000 and 2001.

Impressive test-score improvements by Texas schools were credited to accountability policies pioneered by George Bush when he was governor. They later formed the blueprint for the White House's No Child Left Behind Act. Under the reforms, schools that fail to hit test targets face sanctions culminating in mass firings and closure. In 2005 allegations of cheating in hundreds of schools cast fresh doubt on the 'Texas education miracle'. Cheating inquiries were under way in all Texas's major cities, following a Dallas newspaper probe uncovering huge test-score swings from one year to the next and marked variations across a range of subjects at nearly 400 schools.

Several schools under investigation had been held up as models. Houston's Wesley Elementary was feted by President Bush when he was Texas governor, and by television chat-show host Oprah Winfrey, as a school bucking the odds with at-risk students. Officials were investigating allegations that staff were expected to administer tests 'the Wesley way', prompting students and filling out answer sheets themselves.

The government constantly claim that standards have improved, and quote the 'remarkable' rise in the national test scores for 11 year olds during the late 1990s (between 1995 and 2000 the percentage of pupils awarded Level 4 or above rose from 48 per cent to 75 per cent in English and from 44 per cent to 72 per cent in maths). A study by the independent Statistics Commission cited other factors including the incentive for teachers to 'teach to test', which could be expected to lead to an initial rise in test results, 'even if it does nothing to raise standards'.

The QCA backed the findings of the largest study into national test standards, carried out by Alf Massey of the University of Cambridge Local Examinations syndicate. It found that the pass mark for English was set five marks too low both in 1999 and 2000, because the standard of the reading test fell. The QCA concluded 'The Massey report confirmed that standards have risen, but not necessarily to the extent suggested by the test scores'.

Another report carried out by Professor Colin Richards, for the Association of Teachers and Lecturers, showed that pupil scores under teacher assessment improved more slowly than test results during 1996–2000. In English, test passes for Level 4 rose by 17 percentage points but only by 10 per cent under teacher assessment. In maths, test scores rose by 18 points but assessment by teachers recorded a 12 per cent increase. Richards again concluded that improvements had not been as great as the test scores implied.

Schools used to work together and share ideas and resources, but in the new competitive environment who wants to help a potential rival? Yes, I did hear a head describe a neighbouring school as 'a rival'. Crude league tables also lead to the 'Manchester United syndrome', where people wait for chart toppers to fall from grace – will today's Take Thats be tomorrow's Gary Barlows? Instead of cooperation and collaboration we have the bitterness and enmity engendered by coarse comparison.

The pressure to succeed and the fear of failure is not confined

to education, in sport there's also the justification that 'everyone else is doing it'. Last year the cyclist David Millar was
convicted of taking performance-enhancing drugs, in a
revealing interview he explained why:

> I doped because my job was to arrive highly placed at the
> finish. There were magazines, sports newspapers and tel-
> evision stations waiting for my results ... You dope
> because you are a prisoner of yourself, of glory, of money.
> I was a prisoner of the person that I had become.

In the long term, sport loses out, spectators desist from
attending, after all, they want to see the best competitor not the
biggest drug-cheat winning. Sponsors withdraw funding and
sport self-immolates. The real victims are the athletes, another
cyclist, Marco Pantani, committed suicide after being unable to
live with his conviction for drug abuse.

St Kevin's has languished for years at the bottom of the league
tables. There's been constant pressure from LEA advisers, the
knowledge that Ofsted's first point of reference will be crude
results. Last year they improved slightly. They knew this year
would be difficult, 40 per cent of Year 6 special needs with low
reading ages. Yet low and behold, praise be, after the tests, 85 per
cent of the class are deemed to be Level 4 or above at English.
Exactly how is something of a mystery Pat checked with the
Year 5 teacher to whom she showed her last year's results; that
group was below even Level 3, their reading ages years behind.

Where did this testing psychosis come from? Once again,
America has led the field. There was a report that moves to
reinforce a ban on all formal breaks except lunchtime in one US
city's primary schools left teachers fuming. The law reflects a
broader trend sweeping schools in the US towards dropping
playtime from timetables, to cram students for high-stakes tests.
Education chiefs told primary school headteachers in Tacoma,
near Seattle, that 'with time becoming more precious than
money these days ... there are to be no scheduled daily recesses
... we need to reclaim as much time as possible for instruction'.
Four in ten US education authorities have shortened breaks,
eliminated them outright or are considering plans to do so.

We're no longer pedagogues, the curriculum is out of our control, teachers' autonomy has been destroyed, we're now mere instructors, slaves to the machine. Worse than that, tests, targets and league tables have made us into the equivalent of the cynical doping cheats in sport, our only justification that 'Everyone else does it'. In sport a victory is accompanied by a knowing smile, it's become the same in education. Cheating is so prevalent that even the honest are tarnished.

We encourage children to be open and honest, not to fear failure, we praise success and, where necessary, make constructive criticism. Worst of all is false praise. That's why I can't celebrate or cheer falsity, results that have no resemblance to reality or to children's real ability. But still, rejoice! Get out the banners, summon the press, the target has been achieved! The parents are delighted, the heads relieved and the LEA advisors are ecstatic – their career ladder intact.

Last year one of our teachers attended a training course. During the dinner break the test results were coming out in the schools. Heads furtively reached for mobile phones and then calculators, fevered groups developed working out percentages, and it was a scene resembling Wall Street at its worst. Is this what education has been reduced to?

35 The icing on the cake – the *TES* News Day

We're sitting on the terrace of the House of Commons and it's a blazing hot day. We've brought ten of the children down for *The Times Educational Supplement* News Day awards ceremony. Barry is sitting there looking ill, he's turning a shade of green, after some probing questions we finally ascertain that he's eaten SIX slices of the cake with thick icing.

It's the third time we've tackled the competition; a team of children has to produce a newspaper in one day – local, national and international news, sports, school reports and features. The children have learnt how use catchy headlines, interviewing techniques, choosing stories, editing skills and working together as a team under pressure. For the last two years we've won a Commended award, but this time we've got a Highly Commended. We've improved year by year, and this time with our new digital camera the photographs have really improved.

I send down the reply slip to say we'll be there for the ceremony in the House of Commons. At the same time, I phone our MP to see if he can give us a guided tour of the place. He's really keen about it and says he can get us ten free train tickets. When I ring the number, I'm told they'll be in the post, and blow me down, the next day ten shiny tickets courtesy of Sir Richard Branson arrive.

On the day, the children take enough food to last a week and by ten o'clock we run out of patience and let them start eating. Barry and Neil both have large boxes of Roses chocolates, and start a competition to see who can finish them the quickest.

Getting through the London Underground poses no problems, I'm a map anorak blessed with topographical knowledge. We arrive at the House of Commons and, after going through all the security checks, find the room for the awards ceremony. Most schools have only brought the regulation three children, looking around the audience it's looking a bit like *Top of the Form*, that quiz programme from the 1960s, where very posh schools tried to prove how annoyingly intelligent their children were. A brilliant send-up is Steve Coogan's 'Natural Born Quizzers' which introduces us to trivia nerd half brothers Stuart and Guy Crump. Their only aim in life is to right the wrong that was the 1975 *Top of the Class* quiz final.

A woman with a lapel badge that displays some long double-barrelled name (that is almost certainly pronounced completely differently from the way it's spelt) is looking rather quizzically at us, obviously she's wondering how the ceremony has been gatecrashed by the hordes from Bash Street. After the certificates have been handed out, the MC reveals a huge cake with pink and white icing. He asks if any children would like to get their photograph cutting it, Katie is waiting patiently in front of him. At that moment Mrs Long Double-Barrelled name begins to elbow her way to the front with Daphne in tow. I momentarily forget Debrett's Guide to Etiquette and shout across the room, 'Katie, get hold of that knife'. She's duly photographed with her winning smile in front of the cake. After a few cups of orange and a nice cup of tea, we make it out onto the terrace.

Our MP joins us and takes us on the best guided tour you could imagine. All round the House of Commons, right by the Speaker's Chair, the children sit in Tony Blair's place, then to the red benches of the House of Lords, onto the roof by Big Ben. We see the spot where Charles II nailed Oliver Cromwell's skull and where Thomas More was tried, and William Wallace was executed. The MP is playing a blinder but somehow I think he could talk all day, and we can see the attention deficit syndrome is coming into play and a food-refuelling stop is vital. We thank him profusely and make our way down Whitehall, past 10 Downing Street, stopping to try and make the sentry in the bearskin laugh – but he's heard them all before.

I suggest we find an organic vegetarian restaurant, but naturally I'm outvoted and McDonald's it is. Neil proves what a prodigious appetite he has by consuming a Big Mac with extra fries, a giant milkshake and then does some minesweeping when other children can't finish. Barry just sits there with a glass of water, looking like a doleful bloodhound. We supervise small groups to visit the gift shop next door and they come back with tins of 'London Fog', tacky gifts – turn them over and it says 'Made in Hong Kong' – and my all-time favourite – you shake the ornament and snow descends on Tower Bridge. We had a teacher like that with terrible dandruff.

Next stop is Trafalgar Square, and the children threaten to jump in the fountains, scatter the pigeons and finally climb onto the lions and then across their backs onto the heads. My heart's in my mouth, and after some gentle coaxing we manage to get them down and back to safety.

On the train back I'm reflecting on a brilliant day, everything has slotted into place – the free train tickets, Katie cutting the cake, the tour round the Commons and Trafalgar Square. As we get off the train, Krakatoa finally erupts, a giant stream of vomit propels itself from Barry's mouth. I can see chunks of Roses chocolate, Neil has a grin across his face, and for weeks afterwards I'm picking pieces of pink and white icing out from crevices in my shoes.

36 Bill's new frock – I get to dress up

Every year when we have our school summer fête, the teachers dress up as a character from a children's story. Now, we'd been reading and watching the Channel 4 video of Anne Fine's excellent book, *Bill's New Frock*.

Bill was just one of the lads, 'an ordinary boy with an ordinary sort of life'. One morning he wakes up as Billie and his mum dresses him for school in a new pink frock. His/her life goes into turmoil and he/she starts to see life from a girl's point of view. At school he/she encounters overt sexism – in assembly the head asks for 'four strong volunteers' and picks four boys, of course, 'little girls should be seen and not heard'.

Billie makes friends with Astrid, who can't stand the pathetic boys in class. Rowan Price dares someone to kick the football through the head's open door, Billie rises to the challenge and the enraged head storms out. After Billie owns up, he decides it's an aberration and lets him/her off scot-free – much to the annoyance of the boys. The next morning, to his immense relief, he wakes up as a boy, but his experience has changed his outlook on life.

After watching the film, there was only one choice for the summer fête and I needed a pink frock. Now our local shopping street has the best charity shop in Liverpool. It's in a tough area, but over the years Graham and Derek have become part of the brickwork – local characters. In common parlance they are a bit 'camp', when they have a fancy dress day and come in as pantomime dames – outrageously so.

At some charity shops you bring in a bag of clothes and they barely acknowledge you – 'Put it in the corner and we'll have a look.' Graham and Derek always make a fuss of you, so they always get your cast-offs. The shop is spick and span, bright as a new pin, and they've won a string of awards. They're invariably nattering on about what they did last night, TV soaps and gossiping about the other charity shops. They have a posse of blue-rinse helpers of a certain age and gender – who come in to be shocked and scandalized.

My wife went in a few weeks before the fête and began looking through the clothes rails. Derek came over,

'Looking for anything in particular?'

'I'm looking for a pink frock.'

'Don't mind me saying dear, but it's just not your colour.'

'It's not for me . . . it's for my husband.'

'Oooohhhh . . . Graham come over here. Lady wants a pink frock for her husband.'

'No, no, no . . . he's a teacher.'

'Mmmm . . . didn't have many like that in our day.'

My wife was turning the colour of a . . . pink frock. After a hurried explanation about the teachers dressing up, Anne Fine's book and the pink frock, Graham and Derek quickly found one.

At dinnertime on the day I went into the Gents and surreptitiously changed. I managed to sneak past the door to the dinner hall and into the staffroom. Now our staff can be a bit staid and I had a few glances until one of the younger teachers, Jill, came in and burst out laughing. I went out onto the yard to get the class in. As I strode out there was a near riot, children laughing hysterically, pointing.

The fête went really well, there I was in the pink frock, long hairy legs and Doc Martins. It was just one of those occasions that the children have never forgotten. I'm not so sure about the rest of the staff.

37 'Are we nearly there yet?' – the school trip

These days, we have to justify every activity with a raft of learning objectives (the children will have knowledge of . . .). Not to mention the compensation culture where parents have to sign a five-page indemnity form.

So to keep everyone happy we are on the point of rebranding it as an 'Orientation Exercise', writing a lengthy Mission Statement and spending three staff meetings drafting a policy before sending it on to the governors. In the end we just decide to go ahead and book it any way. Our Day Out! North Wales – Watch Out!

The children arrive early at school with enough food and drink to last a week. Lucy's auntie comes in and faithfully promises to pay on Friday. Lucy looks up at me beseechingly with her milkteeth-rotted, jam-encrusted winning smile. In a moment of weakness I give in – she never goes on any trips. The money never does materialize and I'm in lumber.

The coaches arrive late, 'We got held up, there was an accident.' Accident? We'll believe you, thousands wouldn't, more likely finishing the school run. Four or five children are left gazing forlornly through the window, Jill, who never goes on any trips, and the rest of them not able to make the 'voluntary' donation.

We're on our way and I'm riding shotgun at the front while our classroom assistant picks off any stragglers at the back. Questions, questions, questions, are repeated on a five-minute cycle.

- Where are we?
- Can we have something to eat?
- Can I go to the toilet?
- What's the time?
- Are we nearly there yet?

We arrive at Rhuddlan Castle, the children swarm off the coach, and are soon kitted out with plastic swords from the souvenir shop. They begin to lay siege to the castle, exploring the dungeons, shooting arrows from the battlements, scaling walls, capturing hostages, rescuing fair maidens, torturing prisoners and terrorizing the natives. From the look on the face of the warden, it's clear that the castle has been sacked twice, once by the Vikings and the second time . . .

We gather everyone together and organize races up the steep hill. Teaching point, when they're absolutely knackered they usually don't misbehave. Year 6 go off to examine where the moat used to be. I organize the rest of the juniors. In a flanking movement we climb down an escarpment and plastic swords in hand launch a deadly surprise attack on Year 6 *(Yes, Your Honour, I lifted them all down . . . into the disused moat . . . attacked Year 6 . . . with plastic swords Your Honour . . . a primary school teacher sir . . . 49, Your Honour . . . no it's not my IQ sir)*. By now the warden has given up and retreated into her wooden shed.

We finally round everyone up and drive down through Rhyl. Like most seaside resorts it's shabby, down-at-heel, seen better days, stuck in a 1950s time warp. They used to say about Liverpool – will the last person out please turn off the light? In Rhyl they've unscrewed the light bulb, ripped out all the wiring and nicked the slates off the roof. Sorry Rhyl, no letters please.

We drive down the front, past the boarded-up hotels, the tacky arcades and tired shops. The sea front looks more promising and we disembark for the Sea Life Centre. Inside it's dark and eerie, sharks glide over our heads. We make our way to the education area – a rock pool with seating around it in a horseshoe shape. The children make a beeline for the rock pool. After a few minutes the demonstrator storms in: 'Can't you READ? DON'T pick up the animals.' It dawns on me that empathy with children is not his strong point – he's probably an ex-teacher, they usually are.

He fixes the children with an icy stare and picks up a shell from the pool, immediately a hand goes up. 'Yes, you at the front.'

'Is it alive?'

'Yes, even though it may not look it, it is alive.'

He proceeds to give a long talk about the life cycle of a shell – not the David Bellamy of communication. Next he picks out a crab. A hand goes up at the back. 'Yes, young lady?'

'Is it alive?'

'Yes, it's ALIVE. Everything here is alive.' We get the life history of the crab. They reckon every stand-up comedian knows when they've lost the audience, obviously he's never been one. He picks out a shark's egg. 'Yes, question in the middle.'

'Is it alive?'

'Yes, it's ALIVE, EVERYTHING IN THIS POOL IS ALIVE. THEY'RE ALL ALIVE. EVERYTHING I'M SHOWING YOU IS ALIVE.'

By now we're giving all the children death-ray glares. Finally he lifts out a whelk. There's a question from one of the teachers . . .

'Is it alive?'

He pauses, unable to decide if this is a pathetic attempt at subtle irony, or are all the teachers as dim as the kids?

Through gritted teeth he hisses 'Yes, it's alive.'

We move on to the souvenir shop with the overpriced tack, and feign interest and astonishment. On the beach the tide is out, and it takes a marathon trek to reach the sea. Within two nanoseconds of making contact with the water Wayne has fallen in and is absolutely soaking. Jean and Adele take him back to dry out. Brian's borrowed my Mexican sombrero and looks like an extra from *A Fistful of Dollars*. A breakaway group commandeers the donkeys. Cloverleaf (with Eric on board) makes a bid for Talacre and freedom – Mrs Morgan sets off in hot pursuit. Meanwhile, the shopkeepers just look grateful to see any warm bodies with cash.

We go and find the coach drivers, the two of them are like the characters in *The Odd Couple*. One is laid-back, phlegmatic, seen-it-all before, wouldn't have your job for all the tea. The other one is having a meaningful relationship with his coach, he's constantly cleaning it, brushing the floor, putting out black bin bags and with X-ray vision can spot litter 13 rows back. He later confides that his worst group are the kids from the local public school, 'no pleases or thank yous, not like these kids.'

Back on the coach it's an uneventful journey home, every-one is too shattered to ask questions, argue or fall out. We arrive at school, we've counted them all out and we've counted them all in and they've all come back ALIVE.

An edited version of this article first appeared in the NUT Teacher magazine.

38 Moving on – the interview that didn't succeed

Seven years is enough time in any job, and ten years in *my* school is definitely enough for me. The problem I have is moving schools; like many other teachers, the strains and stresses of a deputy head's position are not for me. So spare a thought for those of us trapped in a school when we just want to move on – it ain't that easy. Teaching in the bleak north, it's not like London where any warm body with QTS is welcome.

The main problem we face is cost – or to put it another way, NQTs, they're everywhere. I've had a number of interviews where I've felt at the end of it – why have you wasted my time? It's true, some schools spell it out in the advert, 'One-year contract – NQTs welcome' – so you don't even bother to apply.

In this particular school there were two posts advertised, and when I got the letter for the interview it explained that there would be a full day – tour of the school, teaching a lesson, dinner and then the interview. When I met the other candidates, there were three NQTs, one teacher finishing her probationary year, and another experienced teacher.

The interview was in early July, and call it sour grapes but by that time the best NQTs have been snapped up. Talking to the other candidates at dinner, let's just say that they weren't going to set the world on fire. In the interview I did my best to talk about my experience as an ICT coordinator and the different projects we'd undertaken in school.

After the interviews had finished, the head came out to say that as he was leaving there would now be three posts on offer – the school is a one-form entry juniors and infants. I thought that it would be between the other experienced teacher and me for at least one of the posts. Imagine our surprise when they announced that the posts were going to two of the NQTs and the probationary teacher. I was really disappointed, the other teacher was inconsolable, she really wanted the job, and she'd been slogging away in a tough school with little support from management.

It was one of those interviews where you come away and think, why? Why? And again why? What had I done wrong? How could they appoint so many inexperienced teachers in such a small school with the head leaving? The next day I rang the head for a debriefing – unusually he volunteered to come out to school the next day and meet me.

I spent the night wondering, had I really made a massive error in the interview? A problem in the lesson? For the life of me I couldn't think of anything. Maybe he was going to put his hand on my shoulder and say 'Son, it's the worst case of halitosis/BO I've ever known, the staff couldn't live with it.'

He came out at dinnertime, 'How do you think it went?' he asked. 'Fine', I replied and smiled back at him. He shifted in his seat and looked uncomfortable. He put my back up straight away because he had no notes from the interview, in fact nothing on paper at all. Usually you get detailed feedback on every question.

He then proceeded to give me two minutes of pure waffle ... 'good interview ... answered questions well ... teaching lesson fine ... references good ...' OK, I've lost out on interviews but at least people have been able to justify it: 'We chose this person because...'

I was beginning to wonder why was this person wasting my time – again. Call it a fault, but I don't suffer fools gladly. I started to ask him some pointed questions: 'What did the other candidates have?' He shifted in his chair: 'Not prepared to go into detail ...' And so it went on with every question I asked, in the end we parted acrimoniously.

I have a friend who teaches at this school, he was surprised when he heard the result of the interviews. Of the teachers appointed, one did well, one just about survived and one was a complete disaster.

Why do schools undervalue teachers' experience? Time and again they appoint the lowest cost option. I'm not attacking NQTs, I used to be one myself, but surely there should be some consideration of balance within a team? I know that you need copious amounts of support in the first year and it takes several years to work your way into the job and gain experience. The figures on NQTs leaving teaching within the first five years bear this out.

Schools are put in an impossible bind because under Local Management of Schools they are only paid average salary costs; the pressure is there to appoint the cheapest, not the best. With threshold payments adding on further costs the difference between recruiting an NQT and an older teacher may range from £10,000 to £16,000.

Before Local Management of Schools it was difficult for NQTs to find jobs, the most experienced candidates were usually appointed. However, the current system leaves thousands of teachers stranded, unable to gain wider experience in another school. Maybe that's another reason why so few teachers apply for promotion.

39 Recharging the batteries – the end of term

In AD 73, the 900-strong Zealot garrison at Masada, a mountaintop fortress near the Dead Sea, committed mass suicide rather than be captured by the Romans. The news that thousands of primary school teachers are leaving in despair may not be comparable, but still shows that desperate people take desperate measures.

It's that end-of-the-school-year feeling, the batteries are low, in need of recharging. Teaching requires tremendous energy, those 20-odd hours in front of the class, you have to be on the top of your game. Some jobs you can have a skinful the night before and stagger into work, you couldn't do that in teaching. The end of the school year is worse for Year 6 teachers, the tests are over and trying to keep the class on task is difficult, 'Miss, we're leaving soon'. Some secondary schools prepare children well for Year 7, others hardly appear through the gate.

There are many days when teaching is still the best job, times when teaching seems effortless, the children are fully engaged on a project, old pupils come back to school and say they loved being in your class. But there are just too many days when the grey mist descends – the all-consuming paperwork; the league tables that place your school at the bottom; the endless government 'initiatives'; the lesson observations from the LEA.

I get news that there's been a staff mutiny at St Ambrose's, the teaching staff have all declared their lack of confidence in the headteacher, and the LEA have sent in a team to try and patch things up. Meanwhile at St Kevin's, as Pat puts it the 'excrement has hit the propulsion unit'. Half the teachers have resigned due to the pressure for results and the headteacher's obsession with paperwork, the parents have been picketing the school with giant placards calling on the head to resign. The LEA can't hush this one up because it's all over the papers.

While teachers are leaving in droves, there are still plenty of new recruits coming up to the front line. The most successful recruitment adverts were the ones showing headless people getting up and going to work. Doubtless there were workers at paper companies in Slough with David Brent as their manager, who pondered the meaning of life and concluded there must be more to it than their present existence. One third of trainee teachers are now mature students, over 25 years of age. However, in 2003–4 14,270 teachers left, 4,180 of them had been in the profession fewer than five years. As the mobile phone companies so inelegantly put it – a high 'churn' rate.

For some of them, the Damascene conversion doesn't last once they encountered the realities of teaching. I read an article by a power station manager who had a mid-life crisis and retrained as a teacher, he lasted one year at a 'challenging' comprehensive. He explained that in his old job he was responsible for 400 staff and he had 10 sub-managers to assist him. When he wanted something done, the entire workforce would respond. The challenge of dealing with a class of 30 where four or five children would refuse to obey even simple instructions and try to wreck the lesson was a completely different challenge, he couldn't handle it and, suitably chastened, went back to the power station.

In comparison with many other jobs, there are still plenty of reasons for becoming a teacher. Pay is not an obvious one, and as with other jobs it's a geographical division, in some parts of the south a teacher's salary is not sufficient to buy a partially insulated rabbit hutch. In the north, the maximum salary of £33k is enough to live comfortably, when you look at the job adverts it's hard to find a comparable one. Remember as well that half the workforce is earning less than £20,000 a year.

The 12 weeks' holidays are a big attraction, although it always takes me at least a week in the summer just to relax, recover and feel like starting a holiday. There's also the temptation to spend all of the holidays planning, marking and, sin of all sins, going into school and doing displays and tidying up the classroom. There was one Teacher of the Year who spent his summer holidays painting his classroom ... sorry, but the holidays are one of the few chances you get to live a 'normal' life, have a few drinks, think about something other than school and be an interesting person.

Even in a job that is defined by routine, by timetables, bells and festivals (Christmas, Easter), there is still variety in every day, the unexpected. Sometimes it's just the weather, what is it about the wind that seems to drive children to the edge of sanity? You can change the routine yourself by introducing something different, organize a school trip, invite a poet or local personality into class, and have a themed day for the whole school.

There's the joy of watching children improve – sometimes you can't see what's under your nose, it's only when you look at the work at the beginning of the year and compare it. Some children barely move on, others leap ahead, that's the ember that keeps on burning, sustains you in teaching: the knowledge that you are helping children to grow, develop and advance.

Working with children keeps you young – primary school is usually one of the best time of times in your life, everything seems possible, you haven't suffered the disappointments of life, there aren't the responsibilities of being an adult, your imagination runs free, the hormones haven't kicked in and before the mould has set there's still time to change. As a teacher, you have your own class and get to know all of your children in a way that secondary teachers never will. Years later, for different reasons there really are children that you will never forget, the nightmare ones, the brain boxes, the daft, the stupid, the insolent, the girl with the lustrous brown eyes, the boy who forgot everything, the irredeemably ugly, the ones you'd want to adopt, the girl who couldn't stop crying, the plain annoying who grated on you like fingernails being drawn across a blackboard, the psychopaths, the confused, the diabetics who tested their blood every day, the ones who reminded you of Ned Seagoon, Sophia Loren, Graham Norton, Frank Carson, any serial killer, Jeffrey Archer, Mother Teresa. Yes, as one paper used to remind us, 'All Human Life is Here'.

If you drew up two columns, for and against a career in teaching, in the against one, for me the paperwork and soul-destroying bureaucracy would feature prominently. The jokes about the consumption of paper, the loss of trees and the effect on global warming are well-worn. My bottom line is – will it benefit the children? I don't begrudge spending extra time on projects that enthuse and engage children, hey we're creative people, but does ticking boxes and endless hours of filling in assessment sheets actually improve you as a pedagogue? The average hours worked in primary schools have gone up from 44 hours in 1971 to 55 hours now. It's the same in most jobs, but as the holidays get nearer you can almost feel the exhaustion setting in.

As an 'intensive support' school (low SATs scores) we have 'support' from the LEA. In years gone by, the LEA had teams of advisors for the curriculum subjects and used well-respected former headteachers to help schools. From 1988 onwards the role of LEAs has been diminished towards almost virtual oblivion. The literacy and numeracy consultants are there to implement the centrally planned curriculum; initiative, independence or any deviation from the set scheme are viewed with suspicion, or banned. Every month there seems to be a new government-inspired 'initiative' that schools are required to adopt – spelling, PE, school meals, history, citizenship. So much micro-management, but schools and teachers are never encouraged to innovate themselves. Then they adopt sayings or catchphrases when a new fashion comes to the fore. When the government document 'Excellence and Enjoyment' came out, it was 'think outside the box', and our Director of Education's favourite, 'be a risk taker'. That after we'd had blanket coverage by various consultants and advisors analysing our planning and observing lessons. Yeah, be a risk taker – sorry, I nearly had my fingers down my throat.

There are benefits and drawbacks from teaching in primary, there's not the horrendous behaviour that can affect some secondaries, but the main drawback is the small staff team. A friend of mine was a fire fighter and they had four watches – red, blue, white and green. You spent all of your working life with this small team, when everyone gelled and got on with each other it was fine, but there were some watches where it was virtual civil war, with no place to hide. In a larger organization, you've more chance of finding like-minded people. In many primary schools the myths of people sitting round in staffrooms with their knitting patterns, guarding treasured chairs and mugs are not wide of the mark. One young teacher I met had worked for five years in a small school with two other staff, both over 50, eventually she'd gone stir-crazy and went on supply.

You do crave adult company at times, someone to have a craic with, talk about the football, what's on TV or just update on the latest gossip in school. It's hard to switch off, when you go on holiday you can always spot the teachers; it's the way they talk to their children. I read about some student teachers who couldn't stop using that teacher voice. One was playing a game with her family at Christmas, and she explained the rules v-e-r-y slowly. Another told her boyfriend to go and wash his hands.

Opinion polls show that 80–90 per cent of parents are satisfied with their children's school and teachers. When different jobs are evaluated the most trusted are medical staff and teachers, the least trusted journalists, politicians and estate agents. The media portrayal is relentlessly negative, children can't read and write, exams are too easy, lurid reports of disciplinary cases where teachers have been suspended, poor behaviour in class, failing schools in chaos.

Part of the agenda is to drive so-called reform, another catchphrase; 'no-change is not an option'. Another platitude that contains a grain of truth, but there's ordered change where you bring people with you, there's change implemented from below, there's change that enhances learning, there's change based on improving resources. Then there's the Chinese Cultural Revolution where you close all the universities, send the Red Guards to attack the professors and ship any oppositionists out to the countryside to work on the collective farms. That was change too.

There are several random factors that can make or break a teaching career. In primary, a lot depends on the class you inherit, a run of challenging classes can be debilitating. There's not even the break you get in secondaries by taking different classes; you're with your class all year.

There are competing pressures in different schools; in a poor area there's the problem with results and league tables, in a richer area there's the parents coming into school asking probing questions about the curriculum from the *Daily Tele-graph Good Schools Guide*.

The danger is that you can slip into supply teacher mode – survive the lesson, survive the day, survive the week. I didn't want to come into teaching to do that. I wanted to inspire children, to light the fire, not fill in forms and tick boxes. I worry that we will be left with the mad, the sad, those people paying off the mortgage and the ever-diminishing number of the downright brilliant. Sometimes the 'Rainy Days and Mondays' have edged out the sunny days. Maybe that's why teachers recite the mantra, 'Christmas, Easter, Summer ... Christmas, Easter, Summer ... Christmas, Easter, Summer...'

Conclusion

40 The road to Hull...

Unless there is a radical change, primary teaching will be like the road to Hull on a bleak winter's morning. You drive through the flat Lincolnshire countryside, mile upon mile of flat landscape, fields monopolized by commercial vegetable growing. An endless vista of cabbages, lettuces, sprouts, all set out in straight lines beneath an unforgiving metal-grey unbroken sky. No trees or hedges break the landscape. You ache for valleys, hills or mountains to break the monotony. Even the rivers and watercourses have been straightened into conformity. The wildlife has disappeared from view and in the depths of winter there's not a human in sight. You're flat-lining; it's grey and bleak, bereft of inspiration. Doubtless the crop is all mapped and monitored by computer to squeeze out every ounce of profit.

Alternatively, maybe it'll be like the film *Pleasantville* (1998). Two American teenagers are teleported into the monochrome black-and-white 1950s TV series 'Pleasantville'. The wholesome inhabitants of 'Pleasantville' appear to glide through life without pain or dissatisfaction, only occasionally pausing for generous helpings of all-American apple pie. However, emotional and creative awakenings spread gradually through the community, destabilizing the established order and prompting the transformation of previously monochrome characters into colour. This new social climate of liberation and free-thinking meets with the disapproval of the local establishment, but eventually the spread of colour is unstoppable.

When Labour was elected in 1997, any hope they would change anything was swiftly extinguished, their first acts were to reappoint Chris Woodhead as head of Ofsted and 'name and shame' 25 'failing' schools. Far from shaking the foundations of the house that Thatcher built, successive education ministers have spent their time throwing in bags of readymix and building shaky extensions (academy schools).

The New Labour mantra constantly bleated by on-message ministerial clones is that 'standards have risen' (independent studies don't reveal the same rise – if any). This is solely based on the increasing number of children reaching Level 4 in national tests, although much to their embarrassment pass rates have levelled and slightly fallen in recent years. Whenever you hear these trite phrases, remember the following –

- From January to April most Year 6 classes will just do revision, taking past papers. They're not learning anything new.
- During that time, 80–90 per cent of teaching will be devoted to maths, English and science – art, music, PE, history are jettisoned.
- Most teachers' and assistants' time (Catch Up, Further Literacy) will be spent on the borderline Level 3/4 children. Special needs, talented and gifted? Stand to one side.
- If your child is bright, they may well be bored to death constantly revising tests they find easy.
- Constant testing reinforces the feeling of failure, spare a thought for SEN children taking tests they cannot understand.
- Every independent study has found high levels of stress among children taking the tests. A Liberal Democrat survey found instances where 7 year olds had wet their beds. Call me a wishy-washy liberal or a hippy child of the 1960s, but that wasn't what I came into education for.

Testing works in symbiosis with the target setting. I've been into classrooms where targets are prominently displayed everywhere, class targets, group targets and individual targets. Gone are the dinosaur displays, the nature table or the author of the month – goodbye creativity, hello utilitarianism. We had a session from our 'consultants' on target-setting in English, every group of children would have targets for can, should and will do – full stops, commas, paragraphs, verbs, nouns, etc. Most schools now have 'optional' tests at the end of every year, another week lost in the curriculum. Some schools then set incremental targets for each child to attain in the succeeding year – 2C to 2A, 3B to 4A. The next step is to tie pay scales through performance management interviews to exam results. In secondary schools, heads can sack teachers who don't achieve results comparable to other subjects.

The philosophy that underpins target setting is that knowledge and learning can be compartmentalized into units. Everything can be measured by testing, and incremental gains are recorded. Knowledge is composed of discrete little bags that can be picked up along the way. In the words of the accelerated learning gurus, 'chunk' everything into little pieces and then test that everyone has learnt it at the end of the lesson. Teachers become so focused on delivering scraps of knowledge that they forget the wider picture, lose sight of imagination, creativity. Children never complete an extended project; they're too busy moving on to the next micro-target.

The final piece in the puzzle is the endless hours of assessment, so children can be assigned a 'level'. We waste time in staff meetings poring over and examining young children's hieroglyphics, they'll be a cry of triumph as someone spies a full stop, and they can move from a 2C to a 2B. I went to a meeting on assessment and a teacher in a special school with the forensic skill of Sherlock Holmes had levelled the squiggles and the scrawls of teenagers with learning difficulties into a portfolio with P8, Level 1 and Level 2. For the life of me I couldn't see any differences. Did it really matter to these children's life chances? Would he have been better employed preparing lessons that were interesting and enjoyable? The latest plans are to level children in every subject, every half term.

It seems that whenever morals or standards are called into question, the kneejerk reaction of politicians is to cry 'back to basics', as though there was some millenarian golden age (50 years ago 80 per cent of children left school without any qualifications and only 5 per cent went to university). The 'back to basics' call began with John Major's speech in 1993: 'It is time to get back to basics: to self-discipline and respect for the law, to consideration for others, to accepting responsibility for yourself and your family, and not shuffling it off on the state.' The campaign was fatally undermined when one minister admitted to having a love child, Jonathan Aitken was exposed as a liar and finally the instigator of 'back to basics' and 'self-discipline' himself had to confess to a four-year tryst with Edwina Currie from 1984 to 1988.

The process of children learning to read has also suffered from the 'back to basics' plague, the most recent example was based on a study of phonic reading skills in Clackmannanshire, Scotland, huge advances in reading ages were reported. Suddenly the magic bullet had been found.

Every reading survey, report, study or review since the sixteenth century has reported that 20 per cent of children have problems with reading English. One of the main reasons is that the written word is not phonetically consistent, blame the constant invasions, blame the Celts, Romans, Anglo-Saxons, Vikings, Normans and name and shame the monks who transcribed the vernacular language. Thousands of words are phonetically inconsistent – one, two, was, want, the, queen, choir, sure, sugar, then there's hard 'c' and soft 'c', hard 'g' and soft 'g', silent letters as in knee, ph is 'f', magic 'e' at the end of words. The Finns have a phonetically consistent written language and don't have the same problems teaching children to read. We've even been there before: the Bullock Report (1975) on Reading concluded that children needed to use phonics in order to learn how to read but they also needed to develop other skills like reading in context and sight memory. The most crucial aspect of reading was to stimulate interest and enjoyment through children accessing a wide range of texts.

Research over a number of years, and in different English-speaking countries, has shown that those children in Year 1, who struggle with reading, and are given intensive support by a well-trained reading skills teacher, will in most cases dramatically improve – this method (Reading Recovery) was pioneered by Dame Marie Clay in New Zealand. There are drawbacks, employing a reading teacher is very expensive and one in five of those given support will still not make appreciable advances.

Instead of reasoned debate, the tone is set (and amplified in the tabloids) by the synthetic phonics zealots of the Reading Reform Foundation, 'People need to ask themselves whether they would choose PREVENTION over intervention. They need to choose what kind of teaching they would prefer for their boys and whether they want to risk their children becoming dyslexic. Quite simply, if you are a parent, to which type of school would YOU most confidently send YOUR children?' 'Quite simply' is always how the 'back to basics' merchants sell the produce. Even the Clackmannanshire report admitted that there was no difference between the comprehension levels of 11 year olds who had been taught 'back to basics' phonics, compared to other children.

You couldn't write the conclusion of a book entitled *How Not to Teach* without coming back to Ofsted. In some ways, because inspections happen every few years it doesn't impinge on teachers' daily lives. It's just always there – a grey eminence, like a stale odour that you can never get rid of, a stain you can't eradicate, that voice that grates inside your head.

What always annoys me is the way it sets itself up as some kind of supreme arbiter, the expert on education, the all-seeing guide and helmsman. I wince every time I read a school that cherry-picks the best quotes from their Ofsted report and uses it on letterheads or publicity. Don't do it! You are only giving these monsters credibility.

But you've got to acknowledge their barefaced cheek and impudence. Recently they warned that speaking and listening skills were being 'widely neglected', because teachers were concentrating on reading and writing. They complained that pressure on pupils to pass national tests was undermining their enjoyment of reading, and small-group work had also suffered because teachers were concentrating on drilling pupils for national tests. This reminded me of the executioner who constructs the gallows, twists the rope into a noose, operates the trap door and in his spare time puts on a kaftan, smokes dope and campaigns for peace, love and understanding – just give up the day job.

The truth is that Ofsted inspections are the modern equivalent of the Potemkin villages – 200 years ago, terrified regional despots given advance notice of a visit by the Empress, erected fake house fronts along the route and deposited well-dressed smiling peasants in front of them. Teachers don't engage in a meaningful, honest dialogue with Ofsted inspectors, not that it pays to tell lies, you just dissimulate, use a terminological inexactitude and are 'economical with the truth'. When you read Gervase Phinn's book, *The Other side of the Dale* (published by Penguin, 1999), you realize that before Ofsted, inspectors regularly visited schools, knew the headteachers well and were, in the main, trusted and respected.

Chris Woodhead began his tenure as chief inspector by calling for 15,000 teachers to be dismissed. Cue headlines, 'Sack These Failing Teachers NOW!' David Bell followed in Woodhead's steps by highlighting failure, accentuating the negative and closing 'failing' schools – '*pour encourager les autres*'. He launched an intemperate attack on teaching in primary schools in the 1960s and 1970s, claiming that much of it had been 'plain crackers'. He claimed that there were 'too many incoherent or non-existent curriculums, too many eccentric and unevaluated teaching methods, and too much of the totally soft-centred belief that children would learn if you left them to it'. Bell used that tried and tested debating tactic, set up a few straw soldiers and then reduce your opponents' arguments to absurdity. Or maybe he was using that military tactic the diversionary attack to conceal the yawning chasm in his own defences.

Just to add an element of farce, in response to its critics, Ofsted organized an inspection of its services – by itself. Amazingly, it discovered that there were no serious weaknesses, value for money was good, its contribution to school improvement was good, and its focus on outcomes, very good. The report identified 'considerable evidence' that inspections had raised standards in schools. A more accurate appraisal came from a survey of staff working at the Ofsted headquarters: one in five claimed they had been bullied, one in three wanted to leave and over 60 per cent said the stress levels were so high they affected their work.

Ofsted's supporters claim it is a fearless watchdog that will scrutinize school accounts and is remorseless in its pursuit of failing teachers. Yet where was Ofsted when it was needed most? In 2003, headteacher Colleen McCabe began a five-year prison sentence for fraud. Police said it was impossible to know exactly how much McCabe had stolen from the school's £3 million-a-year budget, but estimated it to be around £500,000. McCabe became the headteacher at St John's secondary school, Bromley in 1995. As the fraud became more daring, students spent an entire winter shivering as a broken boiler went unrepaired. Rats infested outside classrooms. A video shot by one pupil showed library shelves bare of books.

The school's grant-maintained status (the model for Labour's academies) helped perpetuate McCabe's fraud – the council auditors were kept out. Staff told tales of extravagant flower arrangements in her office, while dirt piled up in corridors, and of crates of empties left after management meetings while staff training budgets were cut. They said they were too frightened to speak out.

And what did the Ofsted report in 1996 say (16 months into her reign of terror) about this latter-day Dotheboy's Hall? Here are the highlights from the report, quoted by the local media and used in its publicity –

- The principal and the senior management team provide strong leadership.
- The level of textbook provision is excellent.
- The college manages its finances well.
- The principal has brought about profound changes ... which have resulted in a marked improvement in the quality of education.

All right, I know, you couldn't make it up.

Something like 95 per cent of teachers still belong to a union – National Union of Teachers, 273,000, National Association of Schoolteachers, 236,000, Association of Teachers and Lecturers, 122,000 and the no-strike Professional Association of Teachers, 22,000. A legitimate question is, why with such high membership density are the unions so ineffective – they don't even negotiate directly with the government over pay. That task is delegated to the so-called independent School Teachers' Review Board (STRB) which makes a recommendation on pay rises to the DfES.

However, the main problem is that unions adopted a version

of American-style business unionism. The unions would attempt to provide a service to individual members – cheap mortgages, insurance, credit cards. And like a credit card company, the only contact between the customer and the head office would need to be over the phone or via the Internet. The result is that many schools don't have a union representative, at branch meetings correspondence is still read out, minutes are recorded, honoraria collected, but the patient is alive not living. In the last elections for the executive of the NUT only 8 out of the 27 places were contested, in the others, candidates were returned unopposed. In the recent General Secretary election the turnout was 21 per cent.

Union officials spend their time (as important as it is to the individual concerned) on casework. But like all compensation agents they cherry-pick the best cases they are certain to win, if yours happens to be complicated or contentious you might be waiting in the pending file. Unions fight the symptoms of stress, but not the causes – Ofsted, long hours, targets, the testing culture. Teachers may belong to a union but they are not part of it, don't attend meetings, volunteer to become branch officials or vote in elections. It's there as an insurance policy if you get into trouble.

The last national strikes were way back in the 1980s. Last year, the NUT balloted primary school teachers on a proposal to boycott the SATs tests, over 80 per cent voted to take strike action, the problem was that only just over a third actually voted – so under union rules, the ballot was invalid. When people in a disaster zone are left without food and water for a long time, don't expect the rescue helicopters to get an overwhelming reception.

Teachers believed that if they shut the classroom door they could isolate themselves from the putrid atmosphere. Unfortunately in the horror film even though the doors and windows are sealed the ectoplasm will still find a way in – through the air-conditioning vents, phone wires and drains. In response to the discourse of derision, teachers have internalized failure, they are to blame personally, they're among Woodhead's 15,000 failing teachers. Or they have submitted to the process of colonization whereby they accommodate themselves to a form of control and colonization creeps steadily into their daily routines.

Debate or discussion is stifled, or controversy is simplified into uncomplicated notions or assumptions. Parents are offered A or B, teacher A will insist on strict discipline, enforce high standards and drill children with 'the basics'. In contra-distinction, teacher B is a hippy throwback from the 1960s, who never tests children and believes they learn by osmosis. Faced with this choice, 95 per cent will choose teacher A. Let's offer parents another simple alternative – teacher A is a stressed-out, results-driven, joyless, unthinking automaton, who implements every government directive irrespective of the needs of their particular class or school. Teacher B is a creative, innovative pedagogue who has the time to develop the potential of every child in their class.

The government has a pathological distrust of teachers, the centrally driven Literacy and Numeracy Strategies have de-skilled teachers. The only training available in many schools comes from the so-called consultants reading out of DfES training manuals. They never attempt to engage in a dialogue with teachers, elicit their opinions or listen to ideas. The tablets of stone are handed down from the mountain – thou shalt not show films, thou shalt thrust grammar down their throats, thou shalt divide every lesson into three.

Faith, hope and optimism are still the vital wellsprings for primary teachers. Without those it is easy to lose sight, to become one of the hardened cynics and sceptics that can infect any workplace. My litmus test of anything is – will it benefit the children? Do endless hours of detailed planning or ticking assessment boxes really help them, or should teachers spend time preparing an interesting lesson? To some extent teachers are obliged to undertake some of the paperwork, but if it doesn't benefit the children I'll do the minimum amount required. What is important is to try and walk the walk and talk the talk, within the constraints invent your own curriculum. That's what I've tried to do with some of the projects I've completed with children. When we filmed our play with the local museum, one nervous child really blossomed and later joined a local theatre group. Now that was worth doing, a child's potential realized and a future interest or career opened up.

In 2002, *The Times Educational Supplement* carried a report on Caol Primary in Fort William, it had been the local 'dump school' that took the children no one else wanted. How did they turn it round? Did they grind the children down with endless tests in order to boost phoney league table placings? Did they overload teachers with tons of useless planning? No, they used art.

In 1992, Rob Fairley, a local artist, started working at the school. He created Room 13. The concept behind Room 13 was to give pupils a level of freedom – artistic, practical and intellectual. Pupils have taken responsibility for their own learning and for the running of their arts studio, to the extent of writing out cheques, making funding applications and attending meetings with potential sponsors.

Older pupils can go at any time during the day to work, or to discuss things with Rob Fairley. The only condition is that they are up to date with their classwork. Part of the Room 13 approach is giving pupils the intellectual skills they need to fulfil their potential in years to come. So, as well as creating their own artwork, they carry out research projects based on a list of eminent scientists, artists and writers.

The *TES* report noted: 'Discussions on everything from philosophy to share prices take the place of still lifes and life drawing. Within the space of five minutes, conversation might veer from contraception to Renaissance gilding, to the trigonometry of a goal in Rangers' last game.' In Room 13 the ideas come first, the means of expressing them follow. To illustrate a lesson on how our eyes work and the way our brain can sometimes tell lies, Rob Fairley once blacked out the windows, transformed Room 13 into a giant pinhole camera and turned the familiar landscape into a huge inverted image on the wall opposite. Maybe they should invite David Bell to visit.

The DfES have taken to producing the *Teachers* magazine, it's a bit like *North Korea Today*. It's chock-full of pictures of the Dear Leader visiting model farms and factories as the adoring masses cheer the completion of all the targets in the 5-Year Plan. Meanwhile, half the country is starving. To say that we need the best people in teaching is stating the bleeding obvious. There ought to be a queue a mile long of people wanting to join. But be under no illusions, the powers of Sauron are strong and are increasing. It will take a bare-knuckle, knockdown fight to save the soul of primary teaching.